DRAWING IDEAS
OF
THE
MASTERS

1912 85ª Galopierende Pferde

Paul Klee
Galloping Horses

FREDERICK MALINS

DRAWING IDEAS
OF
THE
MASTERS

Improve Your Drawings
By Studying The Masters

HPBooks

AUTHOR'S NOTE
I would like to thank all who have contributed to the
production of this book, particularly Mark Ritchie and Jean-
Claude Peissel for their expertise and experience, Marie Leahy
for efficient and tactful editing, Freddie Quartley for her
sensitive design, Ann Gissing for typing an illegible
manuscript, Elaine Scott for library facilities, and Margery
Malins for continuous help and advice.

F.M.

Published in Great Britain by
Phaidon Press Limited,
Littlegate House, St Ebbe's Street, Oxford

First published 1981
©1981 by Phaidon Press Limited

Composition by Filmtype Services Limited, Scarborough,
England

Published in the United States by
H.P. Books
Box 5367
Tucson, AZ 85703
602/888 − 2150

Library of Congress Catalog Card Number 81 − 81664
ISBN 0 − 89586 − 107 − 0

Printed in U.S.A.

FRONT COVER: **Andrea del Verrocchio**
Head of a Woman with Elaborate Coiffure

Contents

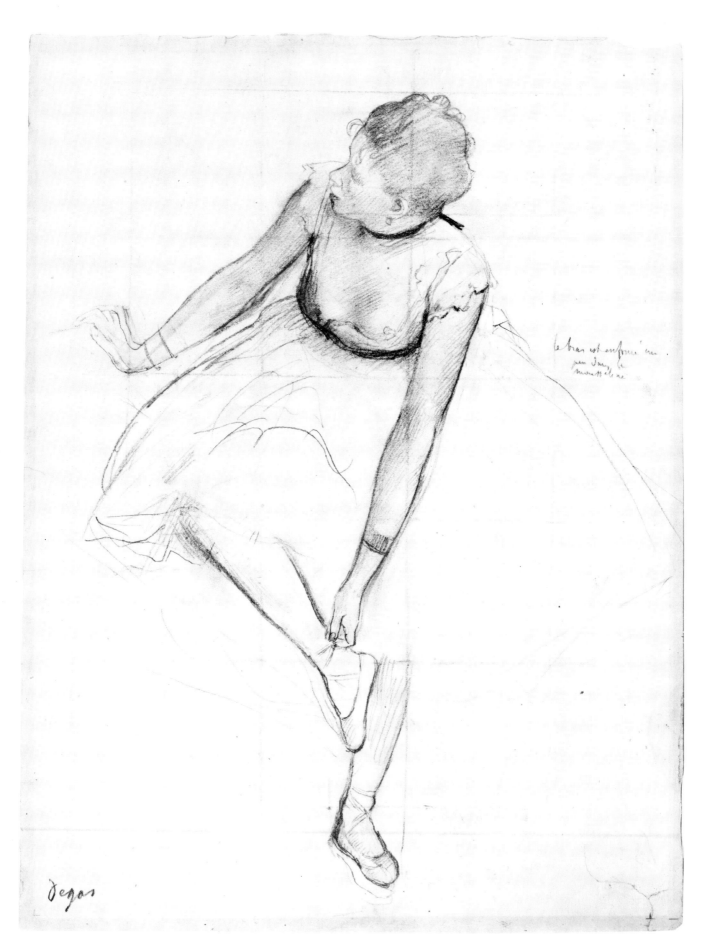

Edgar Degas
Dancer Adjusting Slipper

Introduction

This book is intended to help the reader deepen his appreciation of drawing by studying a selection of works from the point of view of the artist. Although books, slides, films, and lectures are obviously helpful to the student, an appreciation of art is best achieved by simply looking at works of art. Reproductions can play a particularly useful part in a study of the visual arts. This is especially true in the case of drawings, since they tend to rely less on color than other media, are often reproduced in their original size, and, like the books in which they appear, are intended to be studied at close quarters. Furthermore, in looking at drawings we have the advantage of experiencing a direct link with the artist. The marks made by hand responding to eye, however recently or however long ago, have the power to communicate to us directly, without intermediary. In painting the marks have been translated into color, and in sculpture the concept is clothed in three dimensions.

If we study the history of drawing we notice immediately the great variety of media used by artists. We also note the immense variation in the ways the same media have been handled by different artists. To understand more about the material aspect of what is essentially a practical process, there is no better way than to actually make marks, if not drawings, with the various means available. Discovering their possibilities and limitations, and attempting to copy some of the drawings in this book using the same medium as that originally used by the artist, would be a most rewarding and useful experience.

There are three important preliminary decisions that the artist must make before beginning a drawing. First, which medium to use – Wet? Dry? A combination of both? Is the drawing to be in color or monochrome? What surface is it to be drawn on? Paper? Card? White or colored? The choice will be based on the artist's personal preference and experience. Second, he must consider the scale of the drawing and the amount of detail involved. This may limit the range of media at his disposal. For example, if a small sketch is to be made on the back of an envelope (as Sickert used to do on occasion) the medium of charcoal or chalk would be totally unsuitable. Third, the artist must bear in mind the purpose of his drawing. It may be intended to give a client a preview of how a finished drawing may look. Or, more commonly, it may be a preparation for work to be carried out in some other medium – a plan or an elevation for a building, or a sketch for a painting or piece of sculpture. The preparatory drawing may be quite small compared to the final work (a fresco or a tapestry, for example). In this case it is common practice for the drawing to be *squared up* as a means of enlargement when transferring to wall or canvas. You may still see this grid of squares superimposed on the drawing (see, for example, Stanley Spencer's *Elsie Chopping Wood*, Ill. 67).

Where drawings are only a preparatory stage the artist will have the final work in mind when he makes his choice of medium. A drawing for a subsequent painting will perhaps not only show the shadows or light and shade by means of *tone*, but will also indicate the tone *values* of the colors (as in the preparatory studies of Seurat, for example). In this case the artist will choose to execute the drawing in a tonal medium such as chalk or conté crayon. The artist may wish to emphasize the linear aspects – whether seen or imagined – of his subject, for example perspective and the relationship between lines (as in the work of Mondrian). Or movement expressed in linear terms (as in Van Gogh's *Cypresses*, Ill. 96) may be his chief concern. In this case he will choose a medium appropriate for this purpose – reed pen and ink, perhaps. If he wishes to create effects by means of tonal qualities, for example the drama of light and shade (as in a sketch by Rembrandt), or the atmospheric quality of distant mountains (as in a study by Claude), he will be inclined to choose wash and brush, or charcoal. These media lend themselves to broad tonal effects. They are much quicker than laboriously hatching dark areas of tone by pen and ink.

What is drawing?

Let us begin our investigation of drawing by defining our terms. There are as many definitions of the word *drawing* as there are books on drawing, and numerous interpretations of the definitions. The *Oxford Universal Dictionary* defines drawing as "delineation by pen, pencil or crayon," making no mention of brush, silverpoint, pastel or anything else capable of making a mark. By the use of the word "delineation" this implies that drawing is always a matter of lines rather than areas. The *Encyclopedia of World Art* informs us that "the word drawing covers in general all those representations in which an image is obtained by marking whether simply or elaborately upon a surface which constitutes the background." The second definition, which refers to *representation,* opens up a more useful line of inquiry. What is a representation? The *Shorter Oxford Dictionary* devotes forty lines of close print (some 360 words) to an explanation of representation. It says "the action or fact of exhibiting in some visual image or form." This seems to have some relevance to drawing, but the definition "an image, likeness or reproduction in some manner, of a thing" takes us nearer to understanding the meaning of drawing.

To what extent is a drawing a *likeness*, an image or representation of something? Would one drawing be better than another because it looked more *like* the thing it represented? Of course it depends what you mean by *looking like,* and what you understand by a *likeness.* If by a likeness you mean a photographic reproduction, imagining therefore that the better the drawing the more it will resemble a photograph, you may be mistaken. No artist in history has produced a drawing which anyone would mistake for a photograph, nor a drawing which anyone would mistake for reality. Drawing is clearly neither copying nor mechanical reproduction. We should not attempt to assess the qualities of a drawing by referring it to some vaguely remembered faded photograph, some dimly recalled set of visual clichés. Within the context of this work, therefore, the word *drawing* will refer to a creative activity involving skill,

feeling, observation, and intelligence, resulting in a graphic representation of a visual experience seen or imagined. The word *graphic* in this connection implies the use of a medium in which color is of secondary importance to line and form. By representation is meant the creation (on paper or other suitable surface) of a set of relationships analogous to those of point, line, shape, or tone which the artist has discovered by a visual analysis of his subject.

Bearing in mind that drawing is essentially a practical activity, we must appreciate that it is also a means of interpretation and expression. It is important that we understand clearly what the artist is trying to do (for example, when drawing from his observation), and, equally, what he is *not* trying to do. What is he trying to *see* as he gazes at the scene before him? Obviously we need to understand what is meant by *see* and to be able to differentiate between the *seeing* involved in drawing, and the seeing that enables us to move about in our everyday life. (Matisse, when asked if he saw a tomato differently if about to paint it or eat it, explained that if he were going to eat it he simply saw it in the same way as everybody else.) When we understand what the artist is trying to *see* we will be in a better position to appreciate the extent to which he has conveyed his vision to us.

It is of fundamental importance to understand first and foremost that the artist is not setting out to draw *things* (unlike the amateur, who devotes each page of his sketchbook to one *thing,* such as a dog or a shoe). Instead, he attempts to express those visual relationships between points, lines, spaces, and tones which he selects from the chaotic mass of visual information that confronts him in every situation.

The kind of seeing necessary to make a visual analysis is difficult. It is impeded by various factors, and is only achieved by intensive training and self-discipline, coupled with an innate talent. The ability to *see* required for drawing is very different from the everyday *seeing* which enables us to recognize our surroundings, things, or people. In our everyday seeing we are presented with an infinite variety of impressions: images of bewildering complexity and constantly changing patterns that flicker on our retina. Most of the time, fortunately, we are practically unaware of them, sifting and selecting a few relevant facts. We recognize a bus as one we want to catch. We do not notice how it grows in size as it comes towards us. Figures at one end of a room do not strike us as being smaller than those near to us. Most of drawing consists of discovering the difference between what we know and what we see.

In other words, drawings reveal the difference between the appearance of everyday experiences and our preconceived idea of these visual experiences – preconceived ideas which are based on the schematic images we have in our mind's eye, and which have a tendency to superimpose themselves whenever we try to re-evaluate our visual sensations. Hence it is difficult for the beginner to draw a cube with the top (or bottom) on the eye-level so that it presents a straight line, since the top (or bottom) is *known* to be there. Similarly, a child may draw a cup with the top roughly circular but with a flat base since he knows that without this it could not stand up.

This same tendency to confuse what we know and what we see poses difficulties for beginners when they come to deal with foreshortening. Trying to draw a foreshortened arm (which may appear half the length of the other arm) when both arms are known to be of the same length, results in a subconscious attempt to resolve the "short" arm to its known "normal" length. It is thus drawn longer than its appearance warrants. Similarly, there is an innate tendency when dealing with movement in a pose – a twist or a bend – to try to minimize it and restore the figure to the static position "seen" in the mind's eye.

There are still other factors apart from preknowledge, previous experience, and preconceived ideas interfering with our ability to see. For instance, our view of the world may be affected by mood, by our degree of personal involvement or interest. Another important factor intimately related to the idea of preconception is the ability to *name* what is seen. This results in a schematic image being conjured up by that name, thereby effectively interfering with the purely visual sensation. It is well known, for example, that if a group of students is asked to make a sketch of a rather ambiguous diagram, shown to them for a brief period and described as "an anchor" (see Fig. 1) then the results will have more of the characteristics of an anchor than those to whom the same diagram is presented as "a pickaxe." Similarly, in drawing the figure there is the same innate tendency to think in terms of the names by which various parts of the body

are described. The clearly defined line which separates "head" from "neck" in the average beginner's drawing is the result of thinking of (and seeing) the head and neck as separate concepts described by separate words – whereas what is in fact seen is a head-neck complex. In the same way, the black lines around lips, or the individual hairs of eyebrows, are all easily verbally identifiable parts of the head which are pounced on and generally drawn with delight by the amateur, pleased to recognize familiar landmarks. Unfortunately, it is this recognition of objects by name rather than by appearance which gives to the drawings of heads by beginners that peculiar and unlikely character they so often possess.

The final factor which we need to consider in our investigation of the nature of drawing is the role of the artist's "understanding" in the complex process of *seeing*. As Constable said, "... we see nothing truly until we understand it ..." *Seeing* a chessboard or a symmetrical object from the point of view of drawing it will be considerably simplified if we understand that the black and white squares are square and alternate, or, in the case of the object, that both sides are equal. Imagine trying to draw either of the following shapes without understanding their basic construction:

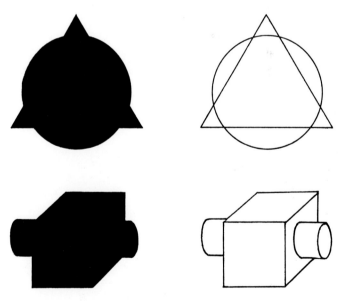

If we understand that a tree may be used as shade or umbrella, that it has grown, moving continuously, though imperceptibly, this will enable us more easily to see the tree as an organic structure. In drawing the figure the artist will realize that the surface form is related to the basic framework of the body. He will convey the realization that certain muscles are flexed,

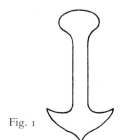

Fig. 1

others relaxed, that clothing is related to forms beneath and that the drapery is affected by gravity, tension or compression. All these and many other ideas are understood and revealed by the intelligent draftsman. His skill lies in analyzing the relationships of lines, forms, and shapes, simplifying complex forms to their basic geometry, organizing multiple tones into three selected values, and conveying graphically and with economy his visual discoveries.

In order to facilitate study of the drawings chosen for this book they have been grouped by subject rather than by technique, or in chronological order. It is useful in learning to develop appreciation to be able to compare and contrast one work with another, a process made more valid when there are common factors. For example, artists drawing the nude must all deal with the subtlety of form and problems of proportion, and the anatomy of the human body.

The choice of artists and subjects is a very personal one. It is based on the author's experience in teaching art appreciation for many years in schools of art and in university departments, and on his experience as a practicing artist. It is hoped that the ideas in the text will not only encourage the reader to look afresh at the work of the Great Masters, but also suggest new approaches and techniques he can explore in his own drawings. Those who are less familiar with the terms used in drawing may wish to study the glossary before going any further. The more experienced reader will probably prefer to turn straight to the text.

Aerial perspective: a term particularly applicable to landscape drawing; refers to a technique of creating the illusion of distance by using lighter tones to represent distant areas, with progressively diminishing contrast of tonal intervals from foreground, through middle distance to background.

Aquarelle: a drawing (or painting) in transparent watercolor.

Aquatint: an etching technique, used to control tonal areas in prints. The name is derived from the resemblance of prints using the method to drawings using water-color washes. This technique is rarely used alone but in association with etching and/or dry point. Goya, Sandby and Picasso all made wide use of aquatint. The traditional method of producing an aquatint is to cover a copper or zinc plate with a fine dust of powdered resin. The plate is carefully warmed in order to fuse these specks onto the plate, thereby covering it with a fine granular surface. When the plate is put into an acid bath, this mordant will gradually eat around each speck of acid-resisting resin dust, thereby creating a finely pitted surface. When printed, this creates an all-over even tone. To control the depth and distribution of tonal areas, an acid-resisting varnish is applied with a brush to stop out the lightest areas after the first biting. Subsequent stopping-out and deeper re-biting can produce a wide range of tones, from the faintest grays to rich velvety darks. There are variations of this process (see SUGAR LIFT).

Bistre: see CONTÉ CRAYON

Blender: a type of brush in which the hair fans out like a shaving-brush, instead of coming to a point; used to blend two or adjacent tones of wet color imperceptibly by stippling.

Body color: opaque watercolor (see GOUACHE).

Brush: for drawing purposes, the sable brush is the most suitable and most commonly used. It is made from the hairs of the red sable, using the natural tips of the hairs to form the pointed end of the brush. A good quality brush is resilient and keeps its pointed shape. Until the end of the nineteenth century and the introduction of the so-called lead pencil, such a brush was called a "pencil." The pointed shape is most common, but flat sables are also used. Second quality brushes are mixtures of sable and oxhair. Badgerhair and dark squirrel, known as camelhair, are sometimes used. Camelhair is soft and floppy. Large camelhair, known as a mop, is sometimes used for blending.

Calligraphic: refers to drawings executed in a free, flowing manner, whether in pen or brush, suggesting the cursive quality of fine handwriting; particularly applicable to drawings by Matisse and Picasso.

Camera obscura: the name means literally "dark chamber" and the device consists of a box (or box-like room) with a small aperture in which a double convex lens is fitted. Light comes through this onto a sheet of ground glass or translucent paper onto which the main lines of the drawing are traced.

Capriccio: a composition that contains bizarre, fantastic or grotesque subjects; also an extravagantly conceived architectural scene or *veduta* in which the architectural elements are accurately depicted but anomalously combined; a *veduta* with purely imaginary elements is called a *veduta ideata*. Canaletto and Robert were eighteenth-century *vedutisti*.

Carbon pencil/Charcoal pencil: a very useful and popular form of black pencil available in different degrees of hardness from soft, through medium to hard; can be used to produce broad areas of tone as well as more detailed linear drawing.

Cartridge: a kind of heavy drawing paper.

Chalk: see CONTÉ CRAYON

Charcoal: a black crayon, usually made from charred willow or vine twigs, available in various degrees of hardness and thickness. Charcoal has been used by artists from earliest times. It is a medium capable of great variety from extremely subtle to rich black and velvety. It is very suitable for rapid work and for comparatively large-scale work. Although easily smudged, it tends to leave a trace of the first impression. It is useful to the draftsman who wishes to carry out revisions and corrections while still being able to see what is being corrected (a process which may be observed in some drawings by Degas). The ability to smudge is used (particularly in nineteenth-century drawings) to create continuous transitions of tone by using a stump or finger. The finished drawing is generally sprayed with fixative.

Chiaroscuro: literally "light/dark", a term applied in drawing (and painting) to describe accentuated light and dark effects. Often dark areas are accentuated to the point where shadowed parts of the form are lost against the dark tone of the background. Rembrandt in particular excelled in this technique.

Chinese ink: see INK

Colored pencils: consisting of unnamed pigments and mixed with clay binder, these pencils are sold in an astonishing variety of colors; none have played a significant role in the history of drawing and they are not recommended as a medium.

Conté crayon: French brand name of crayons which are made in the form of square-sectioned sticks or as pencils. Chalk based, they contain no grease and are available in several colors. The most popular is sanguine – a kind of brick red. They are also available in sepia (reddish brown), bistre (greenish brown), white and black. They come in three grades of hardness (soft, medium, and hard).

Contour: the outline or periphery of a figure (or object); the line that bounds or delineates a form or an area.

Contrapposto: a pose in which the figure stands with most of the weight on one leg, and with the vertical axis of the body in an S-curve; a pose much admired by Italian artists of the Renaissance (e.g. Botticelli) and neoclassical artists (e.g. Ingres).

Crayon: any drawing material in stick form; a stick of chalk or material with chalk base such as conté crayon. The term is also applied to charcoal, grease crayons and lithographic crayons, and is used to describe wax crayons used by children.

Cross-hatching: see HATCHING

Cross-section: often abbreviated to "section" in drawings where the form appears to have been cut through and the face of the cut is visible; more usually refers to an indication of the changing surfaces of a form by means of lines or dotted lines (Henry Moore frequently makes use of this technique in his drawings).

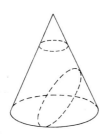

Dragged: describes the technique of brushing comparatively dry paint over a surface so that the color adheres to the raised parts, leaving slightly lower parts untouched.

Engraving: the process of incising a design or drawing onto a hard surface usually of metal or wood, with a sharp tool called a graver, creating an intaglio printing surface. Prints are produced in etching by inking the plate and wiping off the surface, leaving the ink only in the engraved lines – the deeper the incised line, the darker it will print. The technique developed at the same time in Italy, Germany, and the Netherlands, influencing artists throughout Europe (e.g. Dürer, Botticelli).

Etching: the process whereby a design or drawing is eaten into a metal plate, usually copper or zinc, by a mordant – often nitric acid; a chemical process in contrast to the physical process of engraving. The drawing is made with a needle, through a thin coat of an acid-resisting ground, in order to expose the metal to the acid. The plate, back and sides protected, is immersed in acid for a short period, then the lines which are to be faintest are protected with stop-out varnish. The deeper the line is etched, the darker it will print. The plate is returned to the acid bath to deepen the lines not stopped out. The process of stopping out and re-biting is repeated until the required depth of tone in the darkest areas has been achieved. Ink is dabbed into these lines, and the surface of the plate wiped almost clean, leaving the ink in the lines only. The inked plate is printed onto damp paper by an etching process. The etched line differs from the engraved line in that the engraved line tends to be crisper, sharper, and more mechanical in feeling.

Figura serpentinata: exaggerated elongation of the figure into a long drawn-out S-curve.

Foreshortening: the diminishing of certain dimensions of an object or figure in order to show it in a correct spatial relationship. A figure with arm stretched towards the observer, or falling through space (see Michelangelo, Rubens), must be foreshortened.

Golden section: a canon of proportion marked out in the first century BC by Vitruvius to establish architectural standards, and used since in painting and sculpture as well as in architecture. The proportions considered to be ideal are those in which the shorter is to the taller, as the taller is to the whole: approximately 5 units to 8 units.

Gouache: opaque watercolors, usually sold in tubes, containing the same ingredients as transparent watercolors but with the addition of an opaque white.

Graphite: an allotrope of carbon used in pencils. It was not until the eighteenth century that its true composition was understood; previously called "plumbago" or "black lead." This name persisted and today graphite pencils are frequently designated as "lead pencils."

Ground: the texture (rough or smooth) or particularly the color of the surface (sometimes called the support) on which a drawing or painting is made.

Ground plan: positions occupied by forms on a plane drawing (i.e. when seen from directly above).

Hatching: drawing closely parallel lines on a surface to produce a dark tone and thereby simulate the appearance of shadows. Cross-hatching is similar to hatching but uses intersecting lines.

Highlight: the reflection of the light source (often the sky or sun) from the surface of an object.

Ink: drawing ink, usually called India ink, is used in both pen drawing and wash drawing. It consists of carbon, usually lamp black, finely dispersed in an aqueous binder with a wetting agent. It is water-resistant, and when dry may be gone over with wash or watercolor. Chinese ink is similar to India ink but is dried and molded into sticks which the artist uses by rubbing the end on an ink-stone with the addition of water.

Lead pencil: see PENCIL

Linear perspective: a method by which objects are made to appear to recede in space by being drawn progressively smaller. Linear perspective is often shown by parallel lines which recede from the spectator and meet in a point (the vanishing point) on the horizon or eye-level. In practice the rules of legitimate construction are not rigidly adhered to, otherwise a somewhat mechanical effect would result (see Saenredam, Canaletto).

Ochre: earth colors which owe their hue to the presence of iron hydroxide. They are obtainable in a range of hues. If yellow ochres (light, medium, or gold) are heated they turn red and give rise to a whole range of burnt red ochres and earth colors, all reliable in all techniques. These natural burnt ochres, or red earths, are frequently found in volcanic areas as a by-product of past eruptions. Ochre colors are known by various names, including yellow ochre, raw umber, burnt sienna, burnt umber. (Terre-verte or green earth is similar in nature to ochre.)

Pastel: a soft, easily breakable colored crayon containing just enough gum to hold the pigment together. The softer the pastel, the more it is preferred. Pastels are called paintings rather than drawings because the colors are applied in masses rather than lines. Pastels are very fragile and the colors lie on the surface of the paper as a kind of colored dust, but under glass they are very permanent. Spraying with fixative should be avoided since it will bring up reds, ruin tonal relationships, and destroy the characteristic soft quality of the medium.

Pen: originally most pen drawings were made from stalks of reeds or quills; mass-production of steel nibs in the nineteenth century largely supplanted reeds and quills (but see Van Gogh).

Pencil: until the introduction of the lead pencil at the turn of the nineteenth-century, a pencil meant a small, pointed watercolor brush. The "lead" pencil, although very commonly used today for drawing purposes by students, is a difficult medium to handle and has rarely been used by artists in the past, although Ingres and Spencer have found it eminently suitable for their precise styles. See also CARBON/CHARCOAL PENCIL.

Perspective: see AERIAL PERSPECTIVE and LINEAR PERSPECTIVE

Pigment: the basic coloring agent in paint. Pigments or earth colors found occurring in nature have long been esteemed for their permanence and compatibility with other pigments. Pigments which are available as a dry powder may be mixed with gum and water to produce watercolor, or with drying oil to produce oil color. Egg can be added to produce tempera color.

Plane: a flat surface. Forms may be described in terms of planes.

Profile: an outline; especially refers to the face seen from the side.

Profile perdu: a profile that is largely turned away, showing chiefly the contour of the cheek and jaw – a device which enables us to imagine the features for ourselves.

Sanguine: see CONTÉ CRAYON

Schema: diagrams used as guides to obtain "correct" proportion. Geometric schema are sometimes used as a means of drawing the human figure, using an ovoid for the head and spheres and cubes, for example, for other proportions. Drawings from memory must make use of schema, but schema based on years of study and first-hand observation are better than those based on second-hand models. (Although William Blake's schema were fundamentally poor, his personal vision overcame this limitation.)

Sepia: a drawing ink, fairly permanent. Most popular from 1780 to 1880, when bistre tended to be used. Sepia is a warm, reddish brown color, whereas bistre tends towards a cooler greenish brown.

Silver-point: drawings in silver-point are made on paper specially coated with white pigment, using a silver rod as a kind of stylus. This produces a grayish line which becomes gradually darker as the silver tarnishes. Any soft metal such as copper or lead can be used (though they will not darken like silver), and the paper can be coated with white body color which will give much the same effect as the silver-point. Used extensively for drawings during the Renaissance.

Square up: a method of enlarging a drawing. Numbered squares are superimposed on the drawing (directly or on a tracing paper overlay); a similarly numbered grid of larger squares is drawn on the canvas (or other new surface). By noting the positions of lines intersecting the squares on the drawings and plotting these intersections on corresponding squares on the canvas, the drawing may be enlarged to any required size.

Stippling: tapping the color or the surface with the point or tip of the brush or pen as a means of producing an effect of texture.

Stop-out varnish: an acid-resistant varnish used in etching or aquatint to protect those parts of the metal plate which the artist considers to have been bitten sufficiently deeply.

Stump: a light roll of paper pointed at both ends and used to smudge charcoal or chalk drawings to achieve very smooth tonal graduations.

Sugar lift: a variation of the aquatint technique whereby a sugar solution (with the addition of India ink to make the lines visible) is used to draw on the plate. Varnish is applied all over and when this is dry the plate is immersed in warm water, which lifts the stop-out varnish from the sugar drawn lines as they dissolve.

Tempera: refers to a technique of painting in which the pigment is mixed with an emulsion of oily and watery constituents. Eggs, being a natural source of such an emulsion, have traditionally been used, but synthetic emulsions, with vegetable gums or animal glues as the emulsifying agents, have also proved successful.

Three crayons: the technique of using black, white, and red conté crayon to indicate color as well as form. A surprisingly wide range of colors may be suggested by the use of these three alone. Especially useful in figure work (see Veronese).

Tone: a term describing the effect of shadow used to suggest the three-dimensional quality of form; adding "tone" to a drawing means creating the effect of light and shade.

Tone value: all colors have a tone value, according to whether they are light or dark. Tone value is that quality which distinguishes a light color from a dark color.

Topographic landscape: a landscape in which the actual features are depicted as accurately as possible.

Vanishing point: in linear perspective, a point at infinite distance on the horizon line at which lines parallel to each other appear to converge.

Veduta ideata: a scene, apparently realistic, but in fact composed of imaginary elements (see Piranesi; see also CAPRICCIO).

Wash: a brush drawing done on paper using different dilutions of ink or monochrome watercolor. Wash drawings which include the use of pen to define or detail selected areas are called pen-and-wash drawings. It is a difficult technique since a marriage of the two elements is not easily achieved.

Watercolor: pigment mixed with water and gum arabic – the gum causes the pigment to adhere firmly to the paper (or other support). Glycerine (or a similar agent) is used to delay drying and increase transparency – the essential characteristic of this medium. Watercolor is generally used on a white paper so that the untouched white background can be used as light parts of the drawing.

List of Illustrations

Portraits

"Of what consequence is it to the Arts what a Portrait Painter does?" WILLIAM BLAKE

All drawings of heads are not portraits. A portrait deals with the features of the individual (the perceptual), whereas a head is concerned with the general (the conceptual). A portrait artist may choose to see the individual's head and features in terms of three-dimensional geometry. But a head conceived and constructed using the basic building blocks of the cone, cube, cylinder, and sphere is not a portrait – although many great draftsmen, including Raphael, Verrocchio, Leonardo, and Picasso, have constructed some very convincing heads in this way. Portraits may be seen in terms of lines, and heads may be constructed from linear elements (see Klee). Or, again, a portrait may be seen in terms of an African mask (see Ill. 3), though the mask itself is not the portrait, but an invention based on an idea. Neither approach to creating a work of art is more worthy than the other. They are simply different.

All portraits represent a compromise between the personality and demands of the sitter and those of the artist. Artists have generally attempted to show the sitter in a favorable light rather than reflect the less attractive aspects such as the pompous and the pretentious, or the merely pretty or prosaic. There is, though, a danger that excessive vanity on the part of the sitter (or the patron) may result in the weak artist, determined to please, resorting to gross flattery. This is particularly noticeable in drawings of children. There is also the alternative danger, namely that failing to flatter the vain sitter may result in the loss of the commission (or even the destruction of the painting, as in the case of Graham Sutherland's portrait of Sir Winston Churchill).

A certain degree of flattery being acceptable, artist and sitter normally agree that a *likeness* should be the end result. A likeness, of course, is very simple to achieve. Newspaper cartoons and caricatures are sufficiently *like* to be recognizable, but neither would please the sitter or satisfy the portrait artist. Furthermore, there are innumerable *likenesses* of any one of us, as a photograph will demonstrate. Different artists will show us different likenesses of the same sitter. If we compare Rubens' drawing of his first wife with Watteau's version of Rubens' drawing, we can see that a drawing is a portrait not only of the sitter but also of the artist. When the artist is also the sitter we may find 40-odd different self-portraits, as in the case of Van Gogh. All these portraits may well be like him at different times.

There are other problems associated with portraiture as well as those of pleasing the sitter. In the same way that a landscape artist is confronted by the changing moods of Nature, so the human face is capable of expressing varied and subtle emotions. It is for the portrait artist to choose that emphasis which he feels will convey something of the character of the sitter.

Portraiture has always taxed the skills of even the greatest draftsmen. The challenge it continues to offer was aptly summed up by Hogarth: "By perpetual attention to this branch only, one should imagine they [portrait artists] would attain a certain stroke – quite the reverse – for though the whole business lies in an oval of four inches long, which they have before them, they are obliged to repeat and alter the eyes, mouth and nose, three or four times, before they can make it what they think right."

1. Pablo Picasso
Head of a Young Man

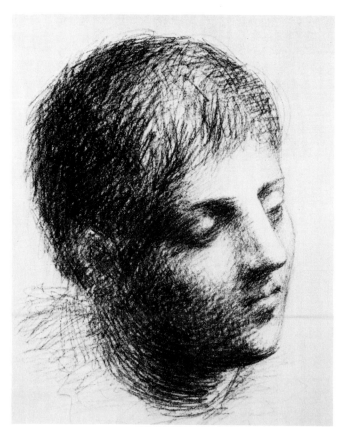

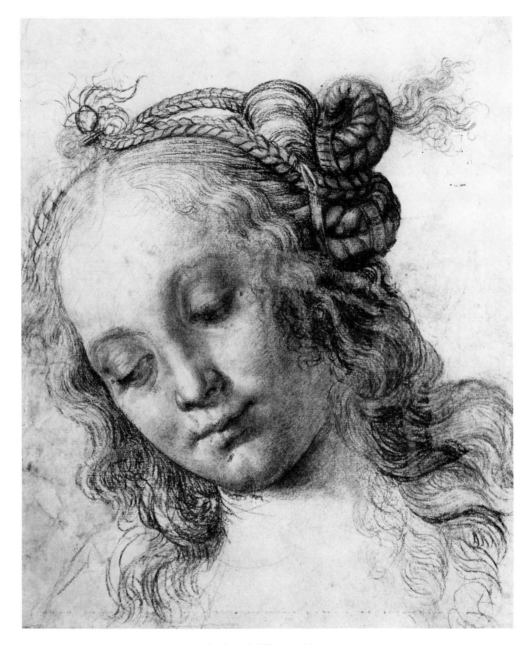

◁ This drawing by Picasso is entitled *Head of a Young Man*. Like many of his drawings, it is an invention freely based on classical models. This is not a portrait of an individual. It is a head constructed from geometric forms, an idea rather than a piece of observation. The head is first conceived as an ovoid form and the directional strokes of the crayon are used to hatch the form into existence, assuming a source of light on the right. This technique of close hatching is somewhat similar to that used by Veronese as in Ill. 24. Where Picasso uses it to create form and lighting, Veronese uses it also to suggest color by means of tone value. Eye sockets are hollowed into the basic ovoid. The eyes are constructed from spherical forms covered with overlapping lids. Consideration is given to the perspective problems involved in assessing relative curvatures of the eyes. The nose is treated as a projecting, wedge-like continuation of the forehead. Smaller spherical additions become nostrils, bottom lip, and chin. The neck is a simple cylindrical support for the head. Unfortunately, this process is not as easy to put into practice as it sounds!

2. Andrea del Verrocchio
Head of a Woman with Elaborate Coiffure

Andrea del Verrocchio creates an elaborately braided hairstyle which helps to disguise the ovoid form of the head. The center part of the hair serves to establish the start of the major axis which runs down the nose and over the lips and cleft of the chin. The minor axes establish the relationship in perspective between the eyes, nostrils, and the line of the lips, and take into account the curvature of the surface. As in the drawing by Picasso, these main forms are lighted from a single source (in this case on the left). Tone is applied to create shadows and reflected lights. Subtle modeling of the surfaces of the main forms allows the artist to convey individuality and expression.

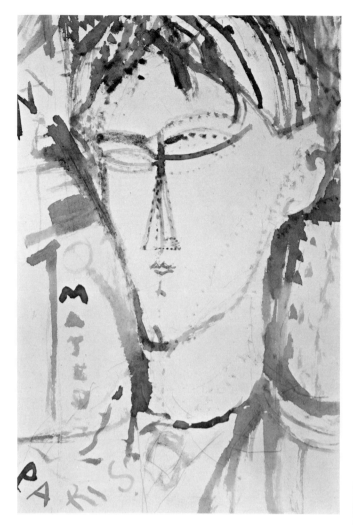

3. Amedeo Modigliani
Portrait of Mateo Alegria

Modigliani's drawing, like Klee's, is very much concerned with lines of varied character – some sweeping, some thick and heavy, some faint and broken. The dotted lines are equally varied, some apparently drawn with the other end of the brush. Like Klee's, this is a drawing of linear relationships. But unlike the former, these lines represent curves, angles, and directions derived from the sitter and his background. The left-hand side of the face sweeps off into the space beyond. The left side of the neck follows suit. These upward thrusts are paralleled by the sweeping movement of the neck/shoulder line on the right, resulting in a powerful feeling of organic growth, which again reminds us of Klee's drawing. However, Modigliani's first love was sculpture. The dotted lines in this drawing are very reminiscent of the marks made by the sculptor's punch as he begins to define the form. Modigliani had seen examples of three-dimensional masks of African origin and his drawing strongly reflects this influence. And yet this is a portrait of Mateo Alegria and doubtless a *likeness*. But this *likeness* is couched in terms of an African mask, with spaces cut out for the eyes. It is rather as if the sitter's appearance is described to us in another language – the language of the Congo, as spoken by an Italian with a pronounced Parisian accent!

4. Paul Klee
Portrait of a Girl Smiling

Paul Klee's work was related to his research into the various roles played by fundamental elements of art – point, line, tone, and color. This drawing explores a particular aspect of line, that is, its capacity to create a sense of movement. The quality of line which Klee employs here is both fluent and fluid. He makes full use of the controlled and contrived accident. By using wet paper to work on he allows the line to spread and grow and take on a life of its own. At this stage Klee steps in, directing and controlling. He emphasizes the eyes. By watering down the wash he softens the corners of the mouth to convey the idea of smiling.

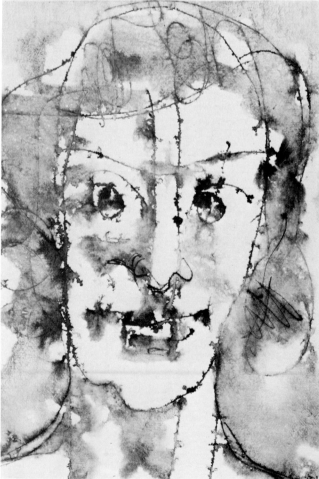

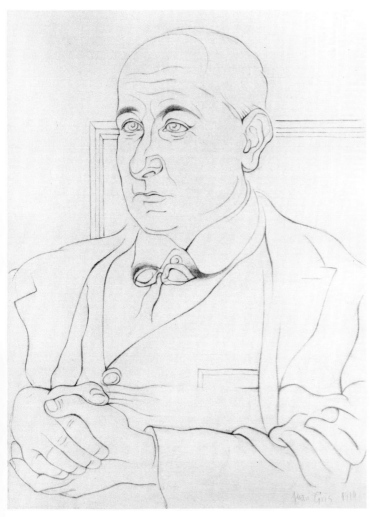

6. Henri Matisse
The Plumed Hat

The Matisse drawing is likewise expressed in terms of line. But though the means may be similar, the purpose is quite different. In this case the emotional content, at once sensuous and decorative, is stressed. All the lines are rhythmically curved and the soft, swinging curves express a mood of pleasant relaxation. "I have always considered drawing *not* as an exercise of particular dexterity but above all a means of expressing intimate feelings and moods – a means simplified to give greater simplicity to expression which shall speak without heaviness directly to the mind of the spectator." The drawing illustrates exactly Matisse's own words.

5. Juan Gris
Portrait of Max Jacob

These two drawings were both carried out in the same year: 1919. Gris represents the classical Cubist tradition and Matisse that of the Fauves (a group of artists primarily interested in strong color and a decorative approach to painting). Gris uses lines to express the structure of the head and is not concerned with the fleeting effects of lighting. The change of plane on the nose and the thickness of the ear and the collar are indicated by linear means. In the background we see the vertical/horizontal structural suggestion, treated in fainter lines than the head. This reminds us of Cézanne's preoccupation with reinforcing the idea of the picture plane by emphasizing the verticals and horizontals (see also Picasso, Ill. 18). The drawing is basically intellectual in approach, and is concerned with the idea of balance without resort to symmetry. The asymmetrical relationship between the eyes and eyebrows is balanced by the two sides of the bow tie, and echoed in the different treatment of lapels. The clasped hands, themselves balancing but not repeating each other, are balanced by the folds of the sleeve on the other side.

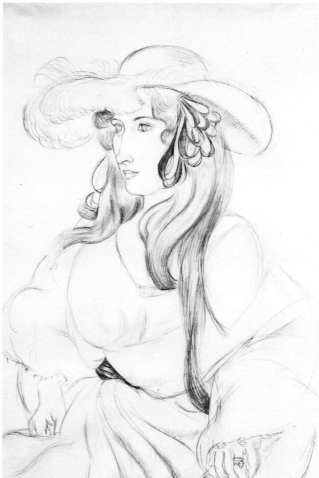

7. Paul Cézanne
Self-portrait

Cézanne would have been hard pressed to make a living as a portrait painter since he worked with painfully slow deliberation, considering carefully each stroke and mark. After over a hundred sittings for a portrait, he is reported to have declared himself not displeased with the shirtfront! Perhaps because of his painstaking approach, he may have found sitters (apart from his servants) difficult to find. This would also explain why he used himself as a model so frequently.

Dissatisfied with the superficial approach (that is, an approach concerned with surface appearances) of the Impressionists, Cézanne tried to re-introduce the *solid and durable*. Cézanne saw his subject – whether a head, landscape or still-life – in terms of its underlying *form*. He ignored the trivialities of accidental lighting effects, or variations of surface texture. To achieve the solid and durable, he used the effects of light and shade to indicate a few significant changes of plane in his subject, not simply to record or describe lighting conditions at a particular time. This preoccupation with form, expressed by an accentuation of the planes, has given Cézanne's drawing a squared-up character. Notice the chiseled quality of the forehead and the interpretation of eyelids as straight lines. This faceted treatment of form (which Cézanne conveniently translated into his paintings using the square stroke of the hog-hair brush) was one of the aspects of his work which was developed by the Cubists.

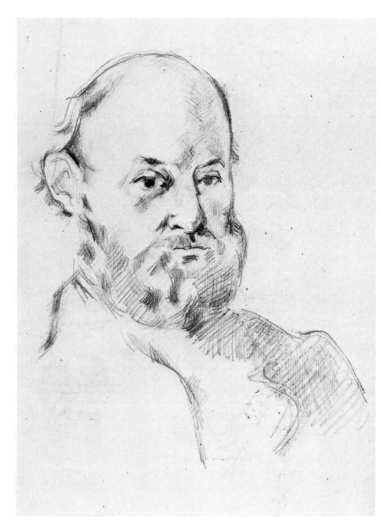

Villon's work, although coming many years later, springs directly from the Cubist vision. However, it re-introduces the sense of light as part of the scene – almost a kind of Impressionist Cubism. This inherent contradiction in terms means that Villon's paintings can perhaps be called exercises in style, since the role of color is difficult to reconcile with the two opposite polarities of Impressionism and Cubism. His drawings, though, are quite clear in their intention. In his self-portrait he sensitively defines the edges of planes by straight lines. The planes are then hatched by straight lines not only to indicate their direction, the angle at which they are lying relative to each other, but also to suggest the effect of light and shade.

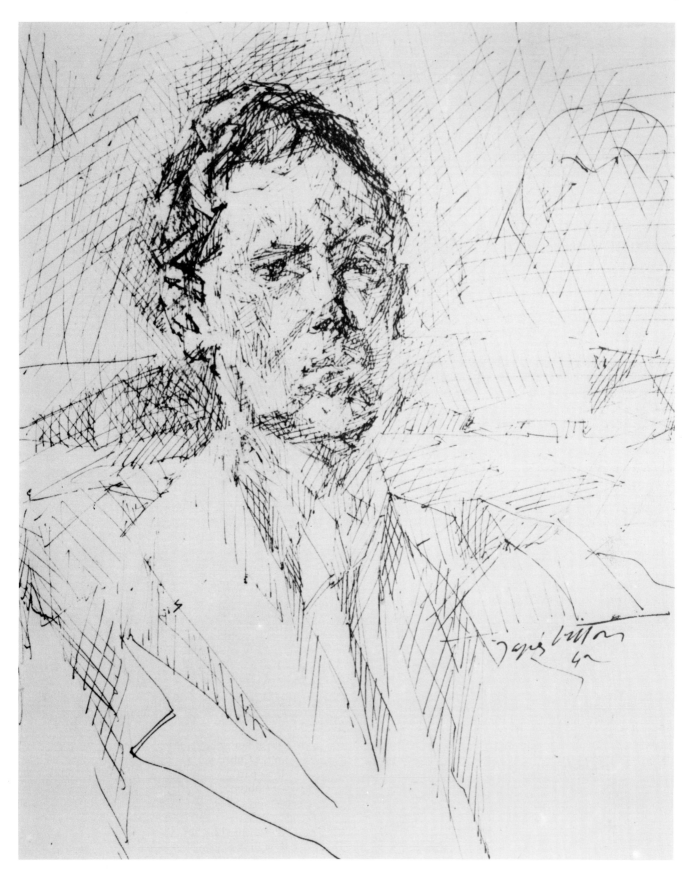

8. Jacques Villon
Self-portrait

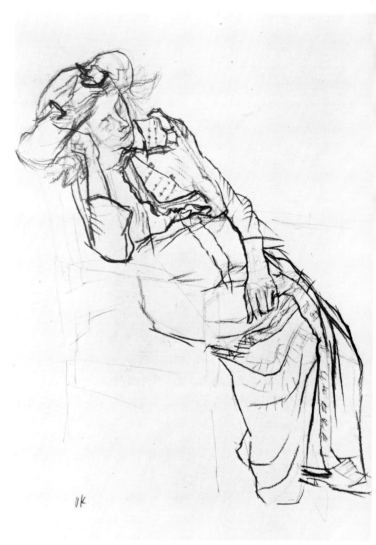

9. Jacques Villon
My Portrait

Portraits, though usually showing the face, are not restricted to the head alone. In his three-quarter length self-portrait of 1934 Jacques Villon shows clearly his preoccupation with the representation of form by means of planes, which he expresses solely by lines. Every form is rigorously squared up and presented in terms of straight lines. Villon also exploits one of the fundamental qualities of line as a means of graphic expression, namely its ability to convey economically and directly the idea of transparency. Lines are used to create overlapping planes, through which we can see other lines. This idea of using transparent planes to express form (a method originally used by Braque and Picasso during their Analytical Cubist period) is exploited further by Villon's use of transparent paper. By tracing one image of the head on top of another and slightly shifting the paper in the process, he suggests that the head is seen from several viewpoints at once, each slightly overlapping the next.

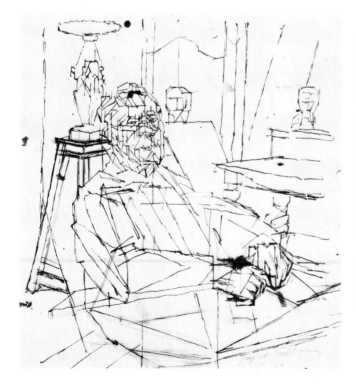

10. Oskar Kokoschka
The Artist's Mother Relaxing in an Armchair

In Kokoschka's portrait the chair is hardly indicated at all, though it is perfectly implied by the posture and perspective of the figure. Like Villon, Kokoschka uses line alone, without the effect of light and shade, to describe the full-length figure. The line travels sensitively over the surface, creating a mood of acceptance and resignation. Kokoschka's line, with its minute changes of direction, is based on very careful observation. On the whole, straight lines predominate, giving the drawing a somewhat edgy quality. There are many very faint lines which are difficult to see in reproduction, but which are very important ingredients. The closed eyes, the internal structure of hands and wrists, and the short lines of hatching on sleeves are included not to indicate direction of light, but to indicate direction of *form*.

One of the chief qualities this drawing possesses, which gives it its sense of authority, is the consistency of its perspective. This is expressed through the use of lines which run across the major axes of the figure (in particular across the eyes, mouth, bodice, and skirt).

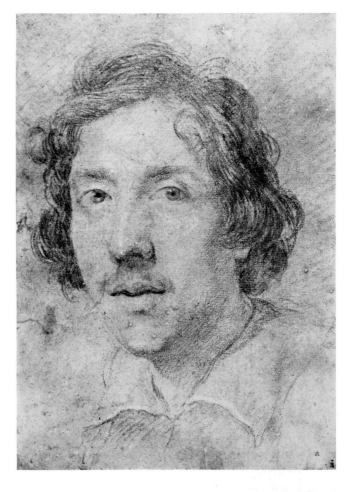

11. Bernini
(a) *Self-portrait*
(b) *Self-portrait as an Old Man*

Bernini could be called the personification of the High
Baroque period. He brought together architecture (he was the
papal architect), sculpture, and painting into one creative
unity, using light as a unifying and dramatic force. These two
self-portraits are very similar in intention and execution,
although separated in time by some sixty years. In each case
Bernini has chosen a left-facing three-quarter front view. It is
easier for a right-handed person to draw this position without
the hand smudging work already done. Light comes from the
left side of the drawing. It is particularly interesting to
compare these two self-portraits, the one by the young,
highly talented 22-year-old and the other by the experienced
old man. Time has brought changes in the appearance of the
face. The hair has receded, the eyes have become sunken in
their sockets, the lines and folds of flesh are signs of age. But
in spite of this, there are more similarities than differences.
For example, the skull, more in evidence as the flesh shrinks,
remains the same bony structure which Bernini had been
concerned to reveal. Both studies are concerned primarily
with *form*. To express this Bernini uses chalk techniques
which enable him to model with ease from very light to rich
dark. He makes particular use of reflected light (a device he
handled with equal skill as an architect), so that the strongest
tone is always along the edge where the form changes plane.

The viewer experiences a curious sensation when looking
at the old man (who is apparently observing us, but of course
in reality was observing himself). We seem to see the young
Bernini gazing out from behind this face. It may be a rather
fanciful suggestion, but perhaps Bernini's quizzical expression,
a combination of compassion, tolerance, and slight
amusement, indicates that he too has recognized his youth.

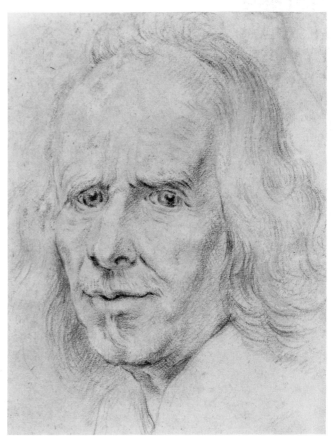

There has been all kinds of conjecture about the appearance of Leonardo. Learned authorities have suggested that his likeness may be found in various sketches. But it is generally agreed that this is a self-portrait of the artist as an old man. Some authorities have suggested that the drawing may be a free copy of Michelangelo's *Moses*, and indeed it has an Old Testament authority and dignity. That the drawing is by Leonardo is not in dispute, nor that it is a powerful and penetrating psychological study.

Leonardo made many careful studies of the anatomy of the human figure, including the head, dissecting and cross-sectioning the cranium in his search for knowledge. In this drawing he concentrates on features, the outer limits of the drawing and the edges of the skull being barely indicated. The roundness of the forehead is conveyed by the way the deep furrows overlap as they travel around and over the contour, helping us almost see *around the corner*. The hair, eyebrows, and beard are rippling movements, becoming imperceptibly fainter as their distance from us increases. Leonardo tended to seek analogies in Nature and universal principles of organic growth. Here he relates the parallel movements of hair to his other studies of flowing water and the swirling movement of growing grasses. The unforgettable expression – particularly in the deep-set, penetrating eyes and in the downswept brows which parallel the down-turned corners of the mouth – powerfully brings to mind Leonardo's disillusionment and frustration in dealing with the vastness of art and life. This frustration is expressed in one of his notebooks: "Tell me if anything was ever done ... was anything ever done ... tell me if ..."

This is a drawing of a character described by Dürer as "a hale and hearty 93-year-old." It is one of a number of similar preparatory drawings which the artist used for his painting of *St Jerome in Meditation* (now in the National Gallery, Lisbon). Dürer uses the very dark purple paper as middle tone and gives equal importance to the handling of dark and light passages, not merely picking out the highlights in white. This structurally solid drawing is largely a study in textural qualities. The dragged, dry, light passage on the cap conveys the surface feel of the material. The headband, we can tell, has a different texture. The bony skull gleams in the light under the deeply furrowed forehead. The rheumy eyes – their expression so different from Leonardo's hawk-like, hypnotic stare – invite our compassion, perhaps even our pity. The coarse texture of the greasy nose contrasts with the delicate fineness of the wispy beard. The beard in turn differs from the hair, drawn in black pen line, which escapes from under the cap. The different kinds of hair are skillfully expressed by different kinds of line.

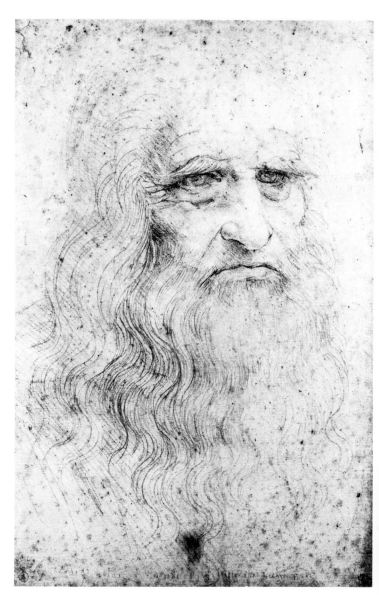

12. Leonardo da Vinci
Self-portrait

RIGHT:
13. Albrecht Dürer
Head of an Old Man

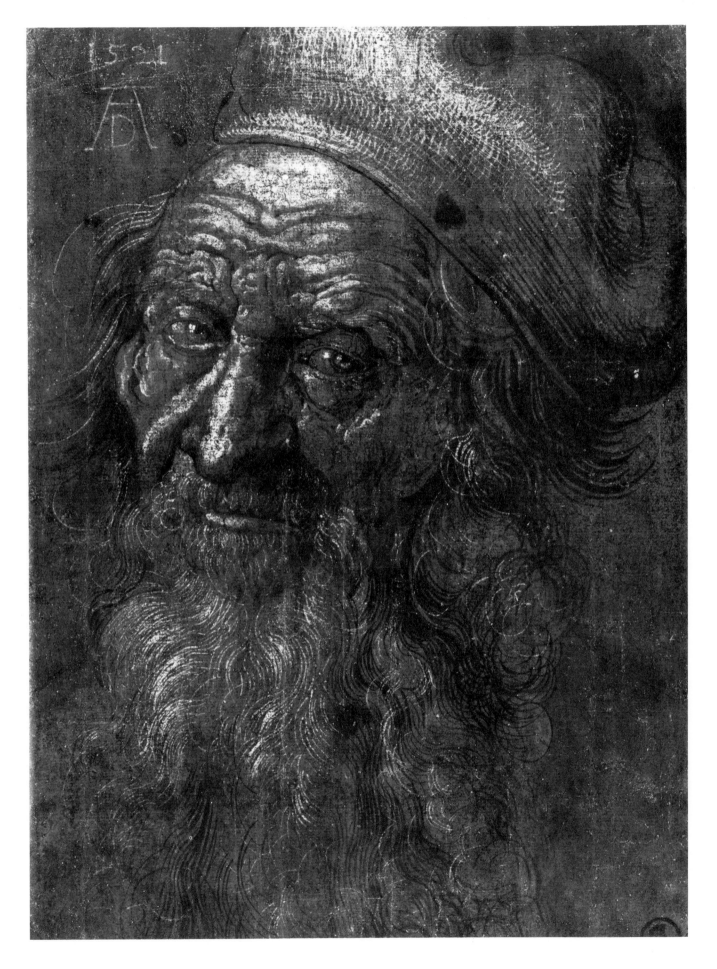

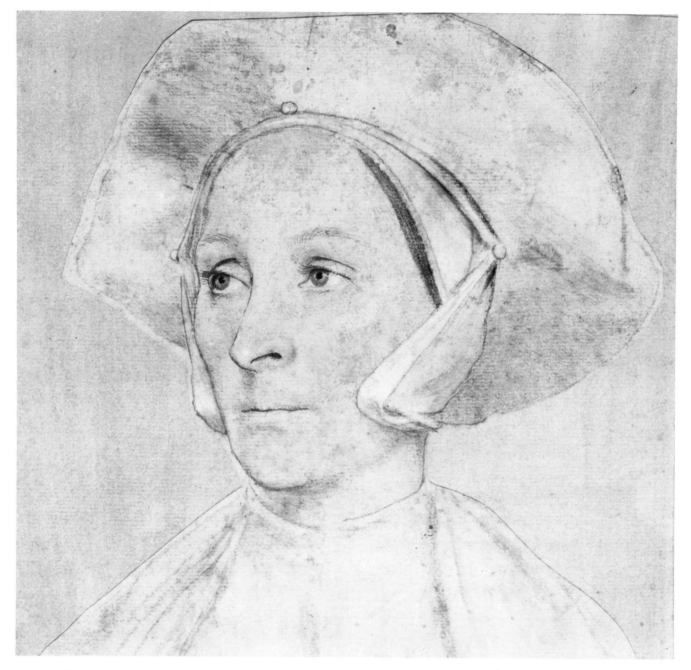

14. Hans Holbein
An English Woman

Hans Holbein the Younger was a contemporary of Raphael
and was much influenced by the Renaissance painters of Italy.
He became Court Painter to Henry VIII in 1538 and drew
and painted all the noteworthy characters at Court, picking
out the distinctive features of each face with authority and
assurance. In this portrait of an English lady in hat and coif
the relationship between the eyes, seen from this particular
viewpoint, is very cleverly realized. The sensitive drawing of
the mouth, with its very slightly accentuated color, is a
triumph of true observation. Tone and color are kept to a
minimum and are used simply to reinforce line.

15. Raphael
Female Saint, half-length

"The essence of Raphael's genius is to be found in his
drawings – he combined rhythmic grace with a subtle but
convincing indication of form and movement." This drawing
by the 21-year-old Raphael precisely illustrates Claude Marks'
observation. It represents classical draftsmanship at its best
and is an example of the kind of drawing that Ingres so
admired. Using a minimum of tone, and relying on subtle
variations of line to create curved sections of the form,
Raphael achieves a convincing sense of softly rounded
volume. The use of tone is so subtle that it is impossible to
decide where it begins or ends, and the use of line to express
the transparency of the headdress is a clever foil to its use in
expressing form in the rest of the drawing.

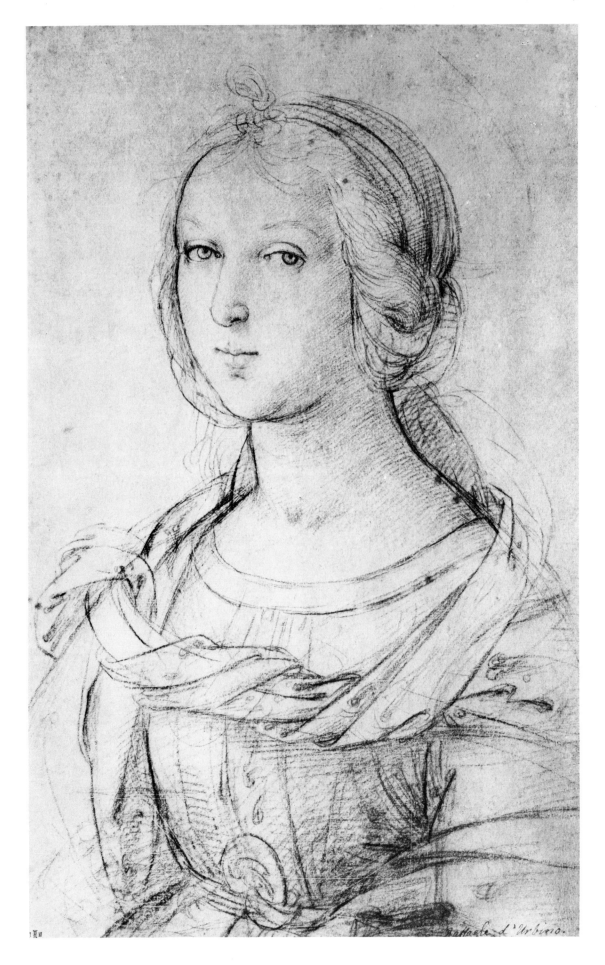

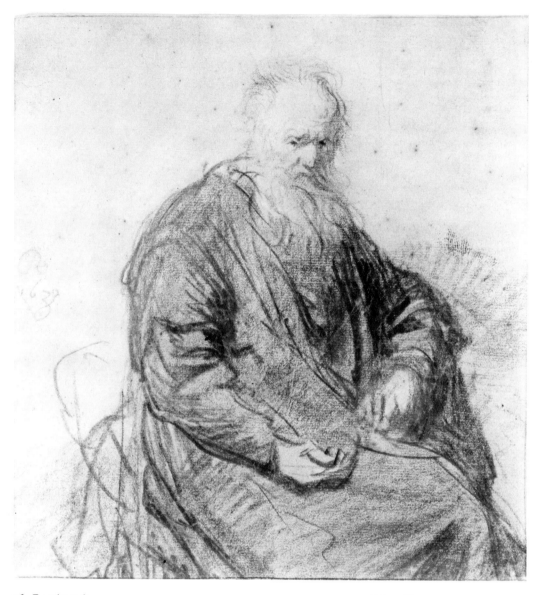

16. Rembrandt
Seated Old Man

17. Edgar Degas
Study for Portrait of Diego Martelli

Although he drew landscapes and animals with equal facility, Rembrandt was essentially interested in the human figure. He is unsurpassed in his penetrating portraits of the old with their profound psychological insight. All his drawings are characterized by his ability to express so much with apparently so little effort and by such simple means. In this drawing Rembrandt calls on the full resources of the crayon from the merest hint to the strongest statement. He conveys not only the shape but also the bulk of the body under the clothes. With only a few strokes he expresses the distance across the front of the figure, between the near arm and the far one, using convincing foreshortening to create this space. Rembrandt's unique ability to produce a feeling of light, atmosphere, and space are revealed in this work. The sense of a single consistent viewpoint is a characteristic of the drawings of both Rembrandt and Degas.

In this study for the portrait of Diego Martelli the artist's eye-level is above the head of the sitter. The feeling of looking down is consistently maintained (consistent because the legs are clearly farther from us than the head). The angle of the implied line joining the twin curves at the bottom of the dark jacket contributes to this sense of looking down by sloping steeply upwards towards the eye-level. As in all Degas' drawings the outlines are simple in the extreme and detail is implied rather than drawn. In this sketch the three-dimensional form of the arm is expressed through the drawing of the fingers and by a few marks on the sleeves.

The use of the *informative* silhouette as a means of describing form reminds us of the importance of Japanese prints on artists of the nineteenth century, particularly Impressionists. Manet used the silhouette of the jacket in his portrait of Émile Zola in much the same way as Degas in this drawing. Silhouettes are informative in that they can express form by indicating cross-sections or by suggesting or implying perspective by means of parallels.

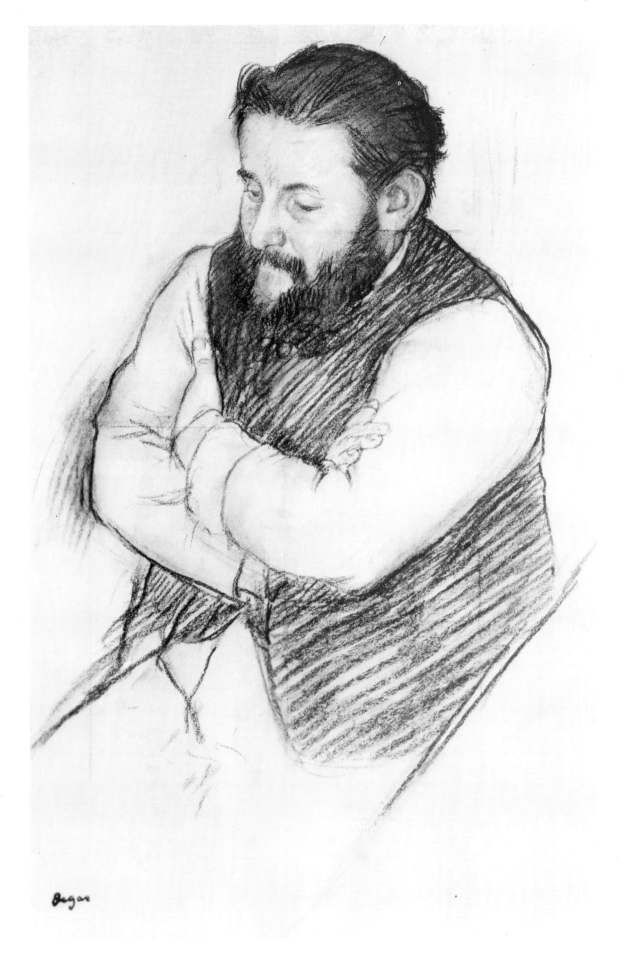

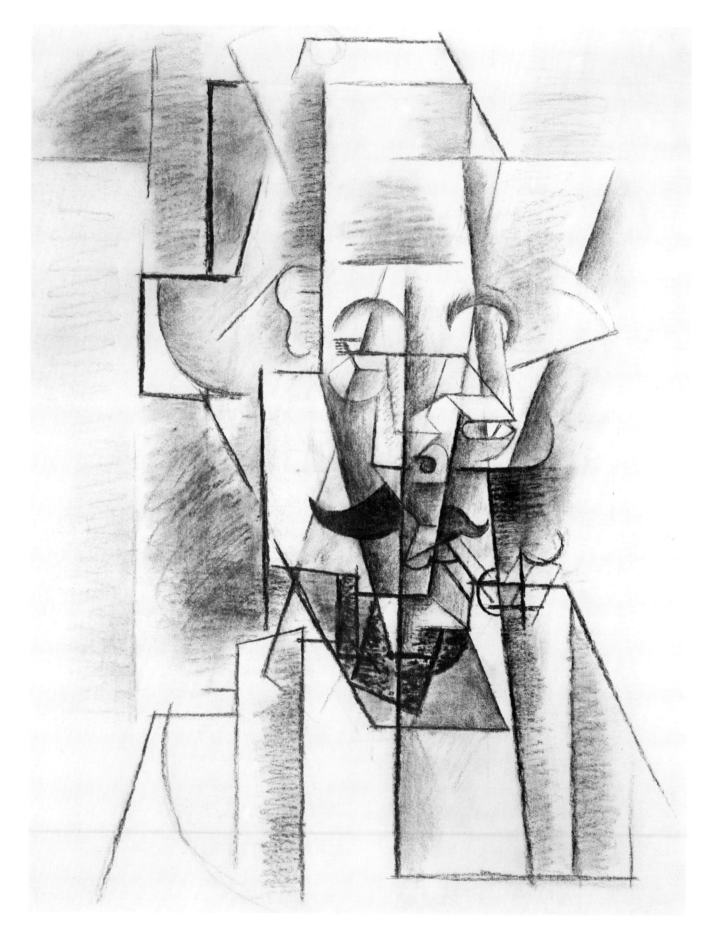

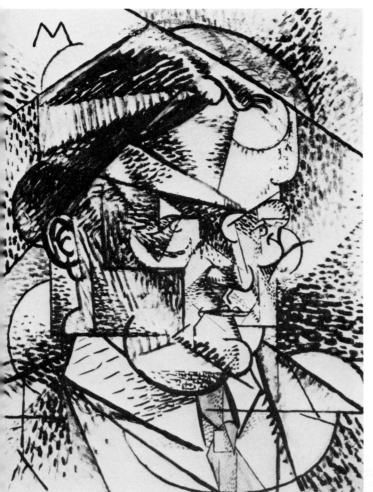

OPPOSITE:
18. Pablo Picasso
Man with Pipe

ABOVE:
19. Louis Marcoussis
Portrait of Edouard Gazanion

These two drawings, both produced *c.* 1912, bear witness to many of the principles of Analytical Cubism. Marcoussis, Polish born, was drawn into the Cubist movement while working in Paris. There, under the leadership of Picasso and Braque, artists had begun to look at nature, landscapes, still-lifes, and portraits in terms of planes. But as we see here, these planes were not necessarily confined to the subject itself. They adopted an independent existence, sliding off the subject onto the background. Initially these planes are defined purely by their linear edges, with correspondingly little sense of depth. The addition of tone, gradating away from these edges, creates a sense of relief. Marcoussis' gradations are of a broader texture than Picasso's, but the principle remains the same. The planes may be seen as in front of, or behind, others. All the time, however deliberately ambiguous their spatial relationship, they still remain resolutely parallel to the picture plane. Although diagonal straight lines are an important element in the structure of these drawings, there is a strong emphasis on a vertical and horizontal framework. This keeps the shifting planes parallel to the surface. These ideas were first used by Cézanne, as was the idea of a multiple viewpoint – the combined side-view/front-view that we find in both these drawings.

OVERLEAF:
20. Peter Paul Rubens
Portrait of Isabella Brant
21. Jean Antoine Watteau
Portrait of Isabella Brant

This drawing of his first wife is one of Rubens' finest portraits. Carried out in the *trois crayons* technique, it illustrates brilliantly the range and variety which this medium can offer – a variety that other artists have also found useful (see Watteau's *Head of a Negro*, Ill. 25). The technique is based on the knowledge that black and white combined produce cool grays for translucent half tones. The addition of red produces a range of warm, vibrant grays. Using this technique, Rubens has achieved a complete mastery of both form and surface texture. We can feel the areas where the bone is near the surface, stretching the skin tightly. The forehead is in itself a masterpiece of surface modeling. The hair is treated with springing curves and the whole head expresses exuberance, vitality, and *joie de vivre*.

Of Flemish extraction, Jean Antoine Watteau studied with interest the works of the Great Masters, and found particular inspiration in the drawings of Rubens. Some claim that a portrait is a portrait of the artist as well as of the sitter. It follows then that Watteau's copy of Rubens, translated into red chalk (his favorite medium), should reveal some aspect of Watteau superimposed upon Rubens – who in turn was revealing his feelings for his wife as well as reproducing her appearance. This is in fact the case. Watteau was a person of melancholy temperament, a consumptive who (like Raphael, Van Gogh, and Toulouse-Lautrec) died at the early age of 37. In his drawing the exuberant, vital Isabella of the Rubens portrait is replaced by a more fragile character. The frankly inviting, direct, sexually appraising gaze becomes, in Watteau's version, a much more ambiguous look. The gaze is directed at a point in the distance, and is more a fond remembering of times past, with sadness just below the surface. Watteau's drawing stresses his spontaneity and emphasizes the decorative aspect of the sitter, thereby reflecting the grace and elegance of the French Rococo. He introduces a rippling necklace to echo the lacy edge of the bodice and lowers the neckline to a fashionable *décolleté*.

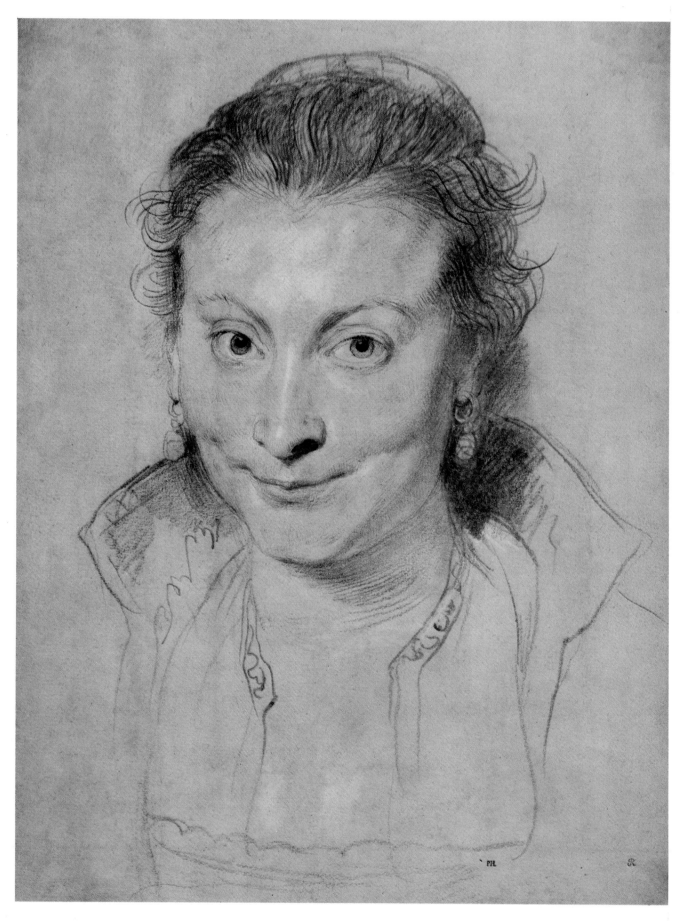

20. Peter Paul Rubens
Portrait of Isabella Brant

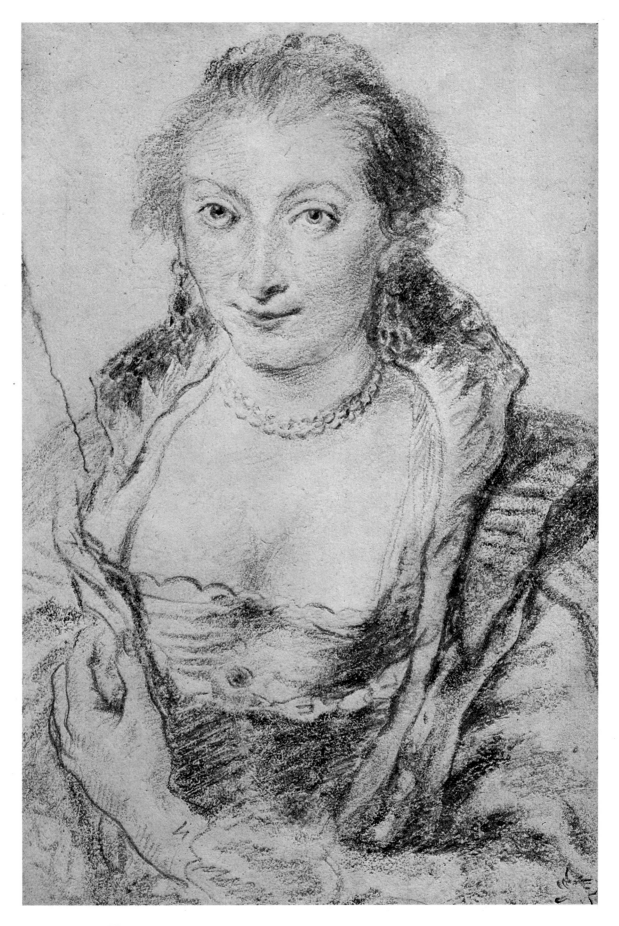

21. Jean Antoine Watteau
Portrait of Isabella Brant

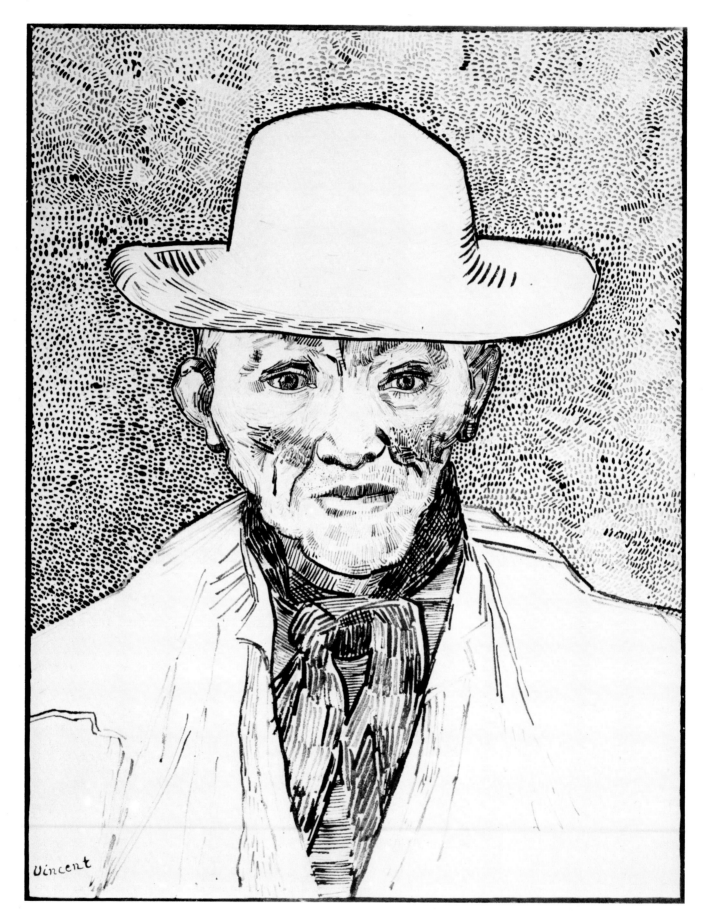

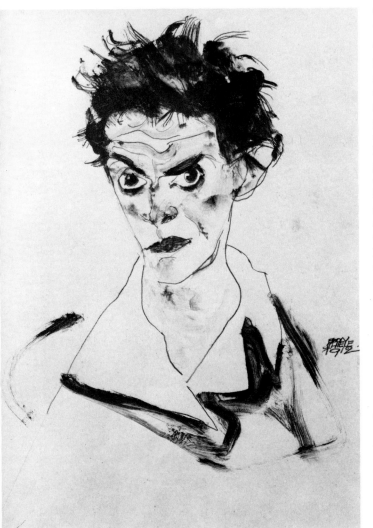

23. Egon Schiele
Self-portrait

To be an Expressionist, to attempt to express one's heightened feelings and emotions about the world rather than simply observe and record objectively, seems an almost certain recipe for disaster. To live at an intensity over and above a certain pitch seems to exhaust the life force prematurely. In his self-portrait Egon Schiele recognizes his own twisted personality and faces up to it. The way in which he uses the watercolor and crayon is almost deliberately graceless. Expressionist artists seem determined not to seduce us by charm of color or handling. They make a fetish of impressing on us the harsh realities of life by deliberately adopting a harshness of color and an ugly, twisted line characterized by abrupt, awkward changes of direction. In this haunted self-portrait Schiele reveals himself, like all Expressionists, the prey of neurotic fears and anxieties. It conveys all those tortured feelings which are the motivation of the Expressionist artist.

OVERLEAF:
24. Veronese
Head of a Negro
25. Jean Antoine Watteau
Head of a Negro

These two drawings of young Negroes are concerned with expressing not only form, likeness, and facial expression, but also the warm color of the skin. To do this both artists have chosen the same means. Watteau's favorite medium was sanguine (he very rarely used a pen for drawing even when copying pen drawings of others: he translated them into sanguine). For this head, though, he has chosen, like Veronese, the medium known as *aux trois crayons*. By working on gray paper he has virtually created the sensation of full color. The head and features are drawn in red, and the shadows strengthened with black. White is used very sparingly to add a glisten to the lips or to highlight the nose. Watteau uses comparatively little red on the turban, only a few marks, using black chalk for shadows. As a result the turban appears white, and contrasts with the dark tone and warm color of the flesh. Veronese, confronted by the same problem, used the same medium but a different ground. Red, black, and white can, in different combinations, produce various colors. Veronese exploits these possibilities. By combining strokes of red and black he produces a brown effect. For local color of lips and cheek he rubs in some red. The solid form of the head is developed by a curved network of chalk lines which describe the shape by following the contours. This profile is an excellent study in perspective. It shows clearly that the outlines of a face are not as if cut out of paper, but skillfully drawn so that some lines appear near (such as the nose lines) and some farther away (for example those over the forehead). In short, the linear boundaries move back and forth in space. This applies to all drawing, but here Veronese has made it very clear to us.

OPPOSITE:
22. Vincent Van Gogh
Peasant of the Camargue

As we have remarked, a portrait may be as much a portrait of the artist as of the sitter. This is particularly true in the case of Vincent Van Gogh. The face of the peasant in this sketch expresses an intensity of feeling which is Van Gogh's own. The twisting, swirling disturbances of the background are a reflection of Van Gogh's own inner turmoil. Indeed, looking at any work by this artist you are always struck by the sheer physical activity and psychic energy which has gone into its creation. Van Gogh uses the brush or, as here, the reed pen, as a weapon – but for creation rather than destruction. Whether he stabs, slashes, flicks or merely punctuates, his movements are always forceful as he strives to communicate the immediacy and intensity of his personal vision. In this drawing he conveys all the glare and heat of the South, yet without having recourse to shadows.

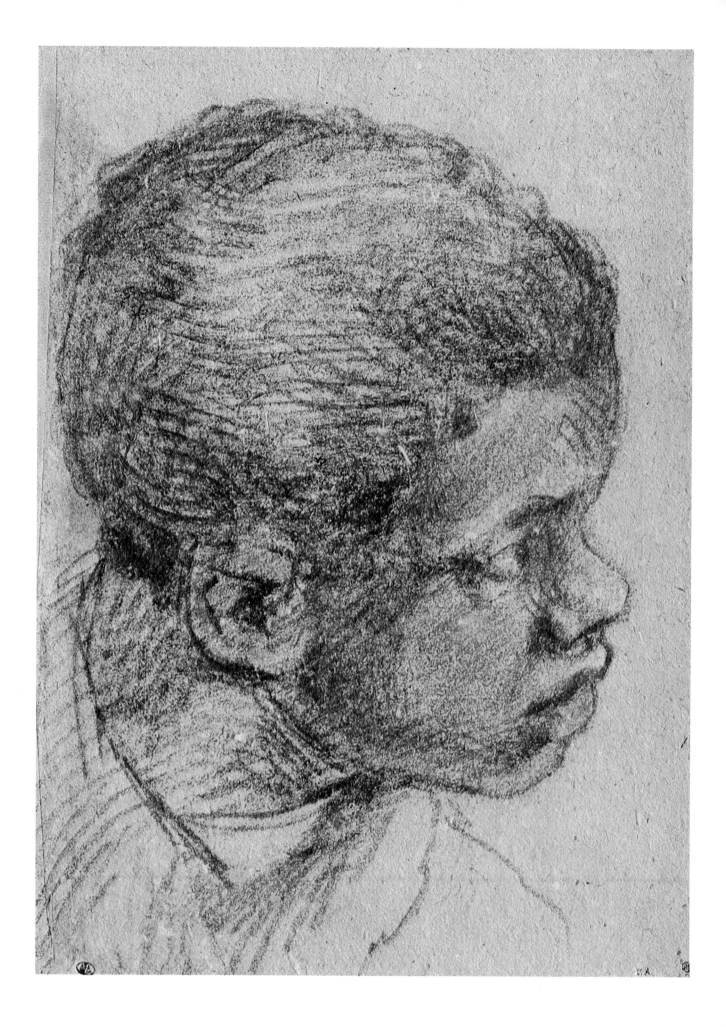

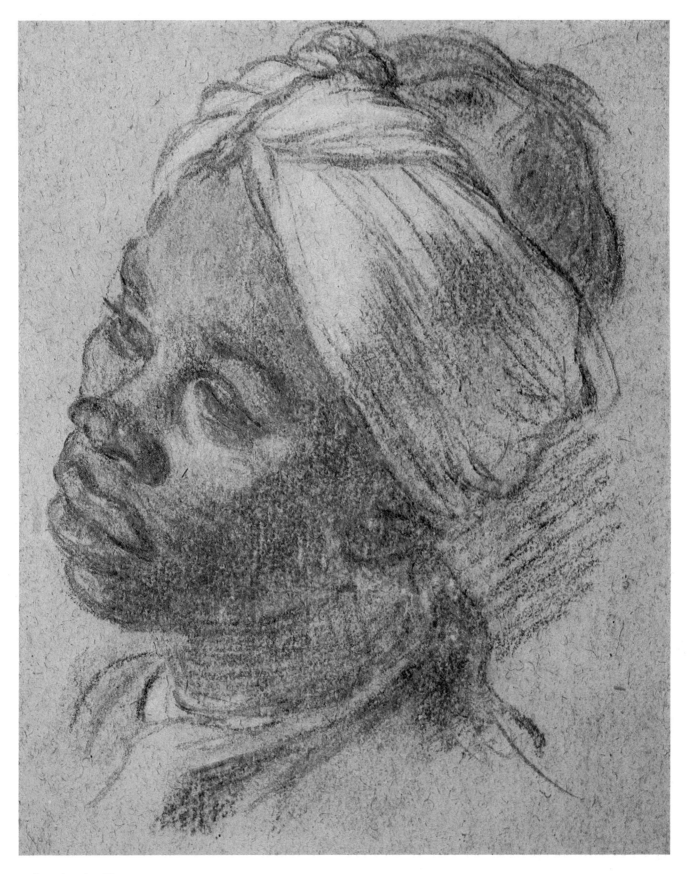

25. Jean Antoine Watteau
Head of a Negro

LEFT:
24. Veronese
Head of a Negro

The Figure

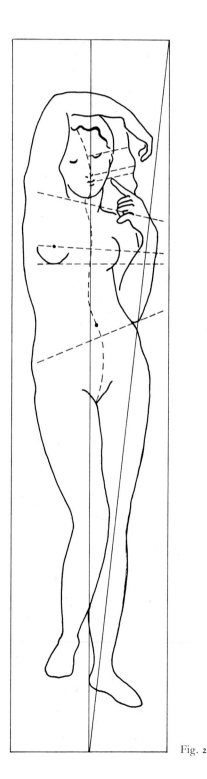

Fig. 2

Figure drawing is a subject which has challenged and fascinated generations of artists of all countries. Every age has interpreted it in a different way. In prehistoric times the female nude was a symbol of fertility. The Egyptians produced a schematic formula which served them well for thousands of years. The Greeks wished to create in their representations of the figure (as in their architecture) a system of perfect proportions. Renaissance artists (Leonardo da Vinci, for example), basing their ideas on the Roman architect and theoretician Vitruvius, attempted to relate the nude to the perfection of geometric form. Michelangelo saw in the male nude the ideal subject, representing God's handiwork.

The changing attitudes to the female nude over the years are reflected in the works of medieval artists. These nudes were characterized by small breasts and prominent stomachs. They are very different from the elongated, fashion-plate studies of the sixteenth-century Mannerists, and the hefty beauties of the Baroque period, with their accentuated curves of breasts, bellies, and bottoms. The swinging curves of the female figure (particularly the back view) were ideal subjects to convey the exuberance and delight in movement so characteristic of the Baroque. A more explicit eroticism – though thinly disguised as Greek mythology – is found in the drawings of French artists of the eighteenth century. But the presence of the nude figure in a work without the pretext of fable or some kind of acceptable setting is very rare before the nineteenth century. More individual and personal styles began to appear in the twentieth century and the popularization of the camera in the 1890s introduced a whole new repertoire of poses for the figure. "Hitherto," Degas wrote, "the nude has been represented in poses which presuppose an audience." Now the *view through the keyhole* suggested an entirely fresh approach.

The particular difficulties associated with drawing the figure are largely due to its variety, complexity and subtlety of form, along with its latent sense of movement. A true realization of the pose is essential. This involves, besides a sense of the space occupied by the figure, an understanding of the relationships between axial directions, disposition of weight, and a sense of those parts which are in tension and those which are in compression. The term *axial directions* refers to the concept of a line drawn from the top of the head downwards through the middle of the body. This line is known as the major axis. Those lines linking opposite points are known as the

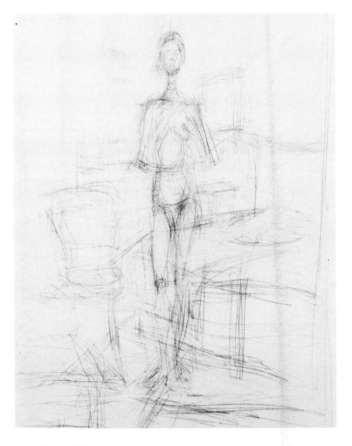

26. Alberto Giacometti
Nude

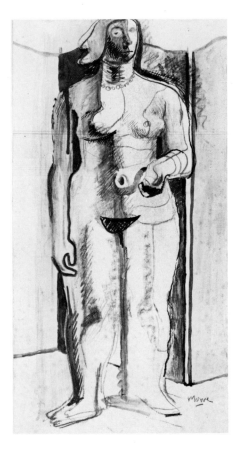

27. Henry Moore
Standing Nude

Both these drawings are of standing nudes, front view. Both are by sculptors of the twentieth century. They are, however, very different both in intention and in method. Giacometti was primarily a sculptor who modeled his figures, creating them from clay. With swift, continuous movements, using a metal armature to support a continuous building process, he clothed the skeletal framework with clay. The result was tall, thread-like figures, as expressive as exclamation marks! This drawing shows a very similar process in two dimensions. Thread-like lines shuttling urgently over the surface weave a fine network, creating the form and pose of the figure. They describe the opposition between the lines of the hips and shoulders. They establish the relationship of the figure to the linear structure of chairs and tables, creating a kind of spatial environment in which the forms exist.

Henry Moore, unlike Giacometti, is predominantly a carver. Where Giacometti's drawing seems to relate to the wiry armature of the modeler, this drawing relates to the basic rectangular block, the starting-point of the carver. Running down the left-hand side of the neck, over the breast and stomach, is a major vertical section which is partially responsible for the four-square quality of this figure. This quality is reinforced by the position of the feet which are planted firmly at right angles to each other. The stance is repeated by the rectangular, block-like form in the background. This form suggests both the figure within the stone block and a niche for a monumental sculpture. Moore uses tone, not to suggest direction of lighting (areas are lighted in an arbitrary way), but simply to convey the idea of form. Similarly, lines are used to show sections of these forms wherever he felt it necessary.

minor axes. In Fig. 2 we see the movement of the central (major) axis compared to the vertical, and some of the compensating movements of the minor axes as the left leg of the model supports the weight. The diagram also indicates the general axial thrust of the supporting leg. In a figure standing rigidly upright the minor axes would be at right angles to the major axis. But such a pose is virtually impossible to hold since the weight must be constantly adjusted in order to maintain the stance. Even the most static pose suggests the possibility of movement.

Before the artist begins drawing the figure he must

decide which aspect he is trying to express and which medium will be the most suitable. Michelangelo concentrated on the anatomical form. Boucher and Renoir tried to express roundness and softness by using a medium which enabled them to achieve smooth transitions of tone. Picasso and Matisse often used line as their sole means of expressing the flow and latent energy of a pose. But whatever an artist wishes to express, he can always find an equivalent in the human figure. It is capable of endless variety and endless interpretation.

28. André Segonzac
Young Girl by a Red Umbrella

Segonzac is probably better known for his drawings and etchings than for his paintings. All his drawings, whether of boxers, women, animals or landscapes (generally winter scenes with a strongly linear content), have a spontaneity and a sense of *joie de vivre* in the way the possibilities of the different media are exploited. In this large drawing the pencil is used sometimes solely as line and sometimes as a reinforcing or modifying tone on the wash. The function of the wash also varies. Sometimes it is used simply to suggest local color (as in the red of the umbrella or the checked pattern of the hat). Sometimes it is used to produce shadow tone on the form. Everything seems to have been done without apparent effort, and the whole casually designed. But from the repetition of the curves of the umbrella, paralleling the contours of the model, to the placing of the signature and message, emphasized by the parallel rippling brush marks, everything has been carefully and elegantly placed.

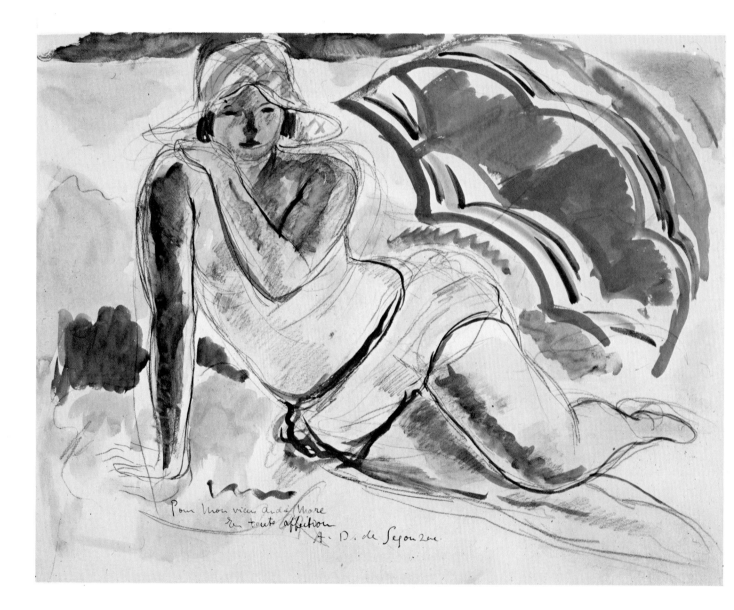

29. Egon Schiele
Wally with Red Blouse

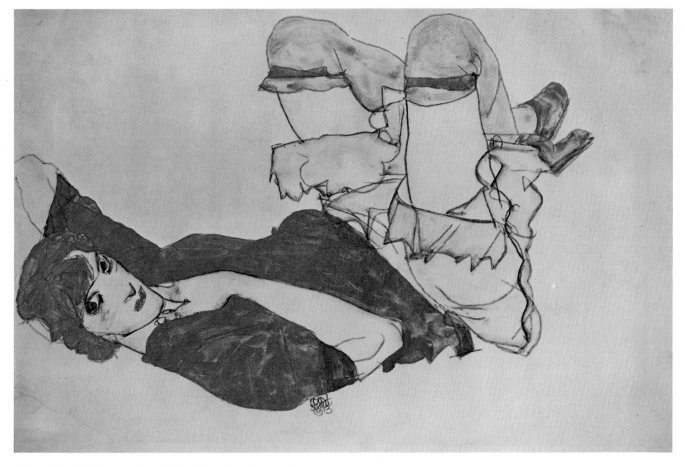

Egon Schiele's line, stark and Gothic in its wiry angularity
(compare Bosch's *Entombment*, Ill. 59), and aggressive in its
insistence on facing up to facts, has none of the elegance and
charm of Segonzac. During his brief career in Vienna, (he
died at 28), Schiele used line as a means of exploring the
human psyche. Like other Expressionists he took a
pessimistic view, tending to see man or woman as the victim
of Life. His drawings of the female figure were much more
naked than nude. The conservative Viennese found them too
explicitly erotic. This drawing, with its flat, stark, discordant
colors (red battling for supremacy with ginger), the abrupt
angularity of pose and line (the turned-back legs of the
drawers are as aggressive as a circular saw), and the
uncompromising gaze, is a typical example of Schiele's superb
draftsmanship.

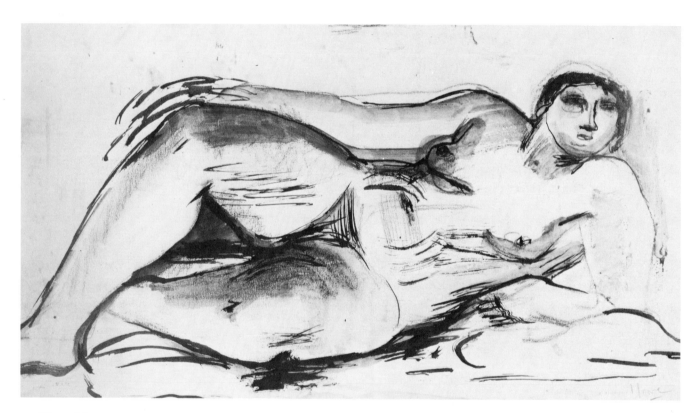

30. Henry Moore
Reclining Nude

The theme of the reclining female figure has run through Henry Moore's work as a dominant motif, recurring in different forms throughout his career. Influenced by ancient Mexican sculpture (such as the reclining figure of the rain god Chichén-Itzá), Moore's drawing of the female nude seems to be larger than life and imbued with a kind of primordial significance. The repeating motif of the parallel straight lines emphasizes the relationship of the massive forms to the horizon, glimpsed as a low straight line between the thighs. By using this idea of a low horizon line the artist conveys a sense of monumentality and permanence. He powerfully suggests an interchangeable relationship between the hills and valleys of a landscape and the sweeping forms and prominences of the female figure, recalling ancestral memories of the Earth Mother Goddess.

Moore uses the brush to produce both line and tonal areas in the form of a simple wash with only slight variation of strength. This tone, like the brief indication of interior modeling in line, is used to show the squareness or roundness of forms, but not to simulate the effect of light and shade.

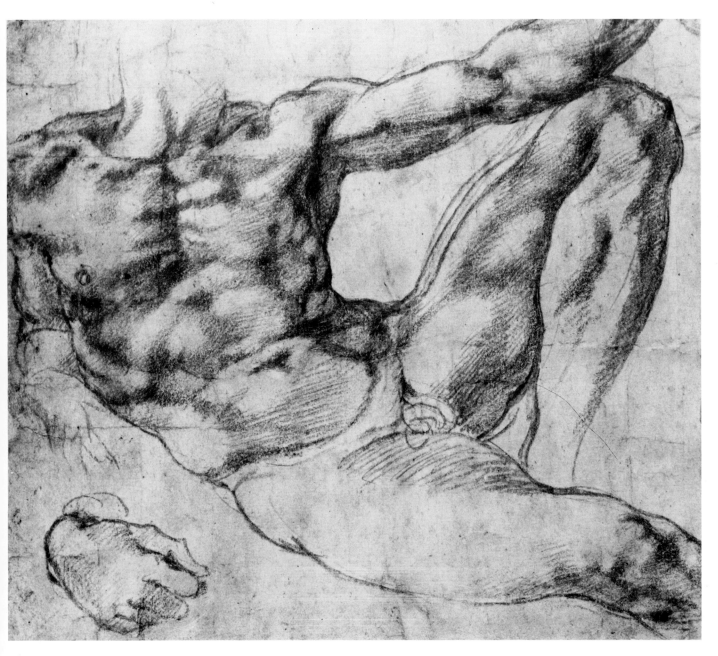

31. Michelangelo
Study for the Creation of Adam

We proceed from the reclining female nude to the reclining male. Here, Adam waits to be called to life. This study in anatomical form was done by one of the greatest sculptors of all time, whose knowledge of anatomy was as extensive as Leonardo's. Michelangelo employs the maximum range of tonal variation obtainable from his chosen medium. He uses the strongest tones on those parts where the form is fullest – that is, where there is a definite change of plane – rather than on modeling up the surfaces of these planes. We can see this method clearly on the nearest edge of the biceps. Similarly, the musculature of the torso is stressed along the lines of the main changes of plane, rather than on individual muscles. Michelangelo's interest was in creating form – an interest one would expect from a sculptor. As in the work of all classical draftsmen, the line is uncompromising and clearly defined.

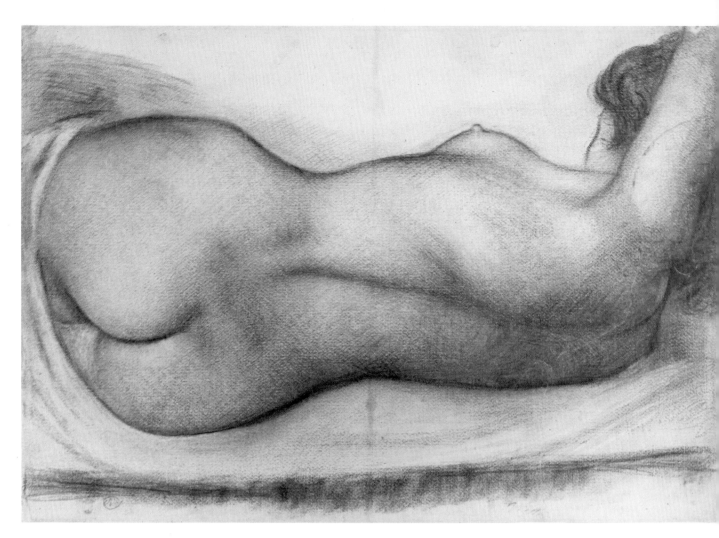

32. Aristide Maillol
Reclining Nude

33. Pierre Auguste Renoir
Nude Woman Seated

The sculptor Maillol began his career as a painter and tapestry designer. He acknowledged freely the influence of Gauguin and Renoir whose pagan devotion to the nude is clearly reflected in his work. Maillol rarely sculpted direct from the model. He preferred to work from large drawings such as this, made from life. "For my taste" he once wrote, "there should be as little movement as possible in sculpture ... the more motionless Egyptian statues are, the more they seem about to move." This drawing expresses precisely a kind of potential movement, a latent activity, more of a sensuous stretching and flexing than a rearrangement of limbs. This sense of arrested movement is conveyed by the subtle twist of the torso. The heavy contour lines of the form roll slowly backwards and forwards in space. The contour of the breast disappears, as it is overtaken by the slowly rising line of the ribcage, which subtly fades and strengthens. The drawing has a definite warmth and sensuality despite the fact that it is virtually an abstract study of form. It is free from details such as hands, feet, or facial features, which often destroy an overall concept of form.

This drawing probably dates from 1885-90 when Renoir, having visited Italy in the winter of 1881-2, *rediscovered* the classical Ingres (see Ill.34) through his study of the works of Raphael. As a result Renoir rejected the Impressionists' total preoccupation with light to the exclusion of form, and acknowledged the prime importance of draftsmanship. Thereafter his drawings took on a monumental sculptural quality which shows his admiration of the surcharged immobility of Maillol's rigidly controlled figures. Like Maillol, Renoir uses strong, firm, simple contours. All the interior forms are modeled within these controlled lines. The detail is subordinate to the whole, fingers being drawn as hand, and facial features largely lost. In this drawing the use of red chalk heightened with white gives the flesh a rosy color, in keeping with the obvious delight with which Renoir has expressed the firm expanse of buttocks, rounded breast, and thigh. The rotation of the shoulder mass, as the model leans over to the foot, compared with the angle of the hips, is particularly masterful.

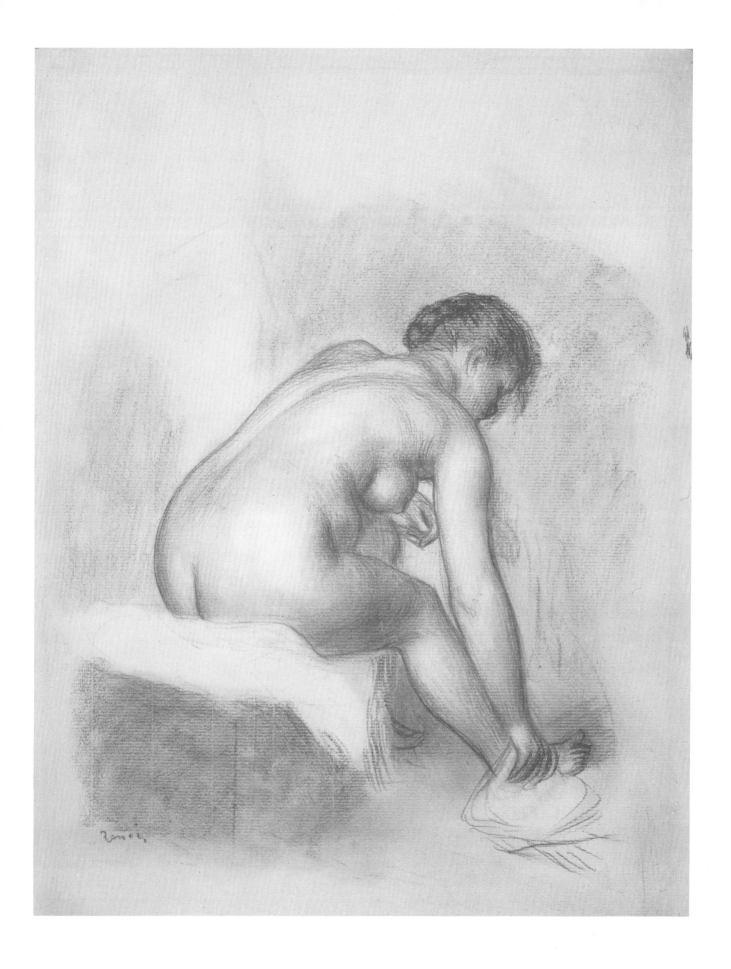

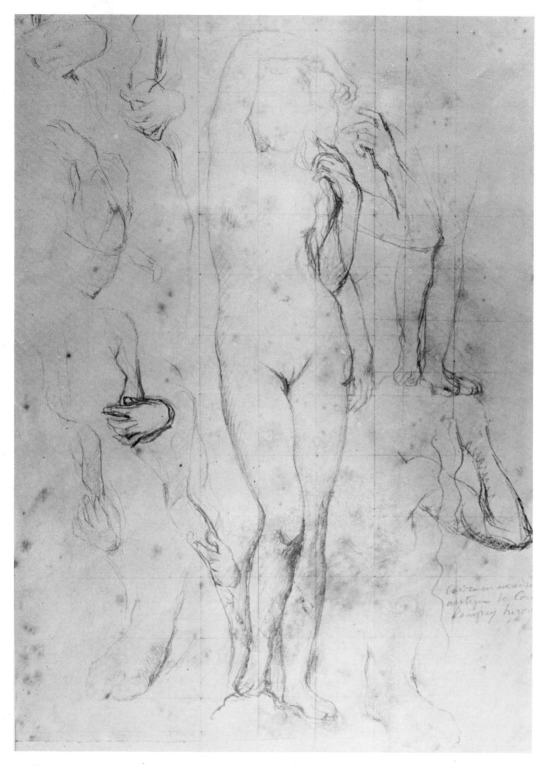

34. Jean Auguste Ingres
Nude Study

Ingres' drawing of a female nude is also a preparatory study. He has squared it up ready for transfer to the canvas. Ingres' use of pencil reminds us of the medieval silver-point, but he has been able to achieve much more flexibility and variety with the new medium (see glossary). In 1806 Ingres left France for Italy, intending to stay a few years but in fact remaining for eighteen. Although he proclaimed an undying admiration for Raphael, behind the cool neoclassical façade there is a feeling of romantic sensuality. This fluid pose, with the subtly swaying movement of the central axis of the figure, accentuates the quality of grace in a way much more associated with the Italian Mannerists (for example Bronzino) than with Raphael. Ingres insisted on the importance of line and drawing, saying "draftsmanship is the probity of Art – line is drawing ... It is everything." But Ingres' line is not everything in this drawing. The line is complemented, subtly modeled, and varied by the addition of tone, which changes in weight as it moves from one side of the line to the other.

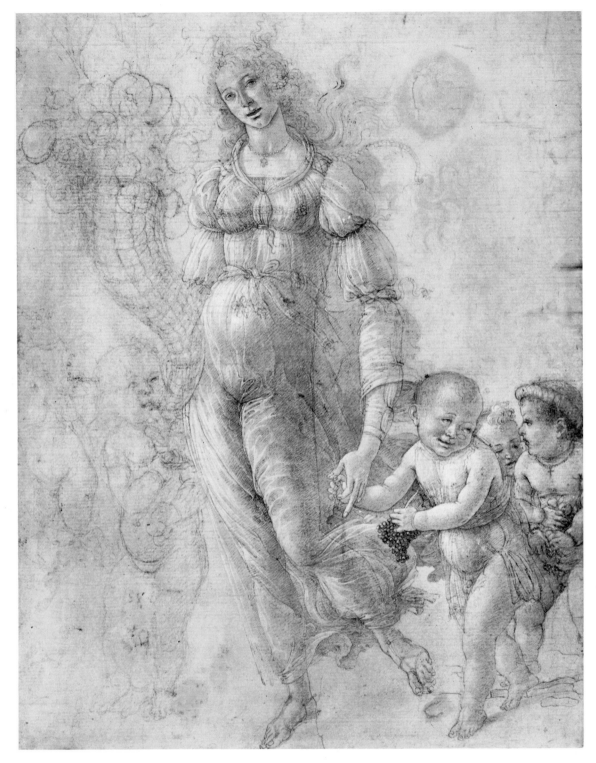

35. Botticelli
Abundance

The paintings of Sandro Botticelli are imbued with a sense of nostalgia and dreaminess. In this beautiful drawing, a preparatory study for one of his works, we can see how he achieves both a sense of movement and a subtle transparency. Botticelli chose to work on a middle-tone ground with pen, chalk, and wash, heightening the drawing with white. This is the ideal combination of media to express delicacy and to bring out the transparency of the drapery. This feeling of delicacy enhances the sense of movement, which is underlined by the floating ribbons and windswept hair, and by the feet, which are hardly in contact with the ground. Botticelli's use of line is soft and caressing. The central axis of the principal figure describes a softly swinging curve. This is echoed in the curve of the cornucopia (a thinly veiled allusion to the idea of fertility suggested by the figure).

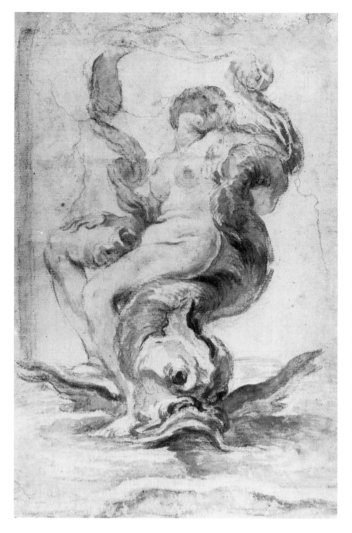

36. Bernini
Study for a Fountain

One of the qualities of High Baroque sculpture is that it appears to deny the nature of the sculptural medium itself. The heaviness and solidity of marble, stone, and bronze are transformed. Even the human body can become ethereal, simply an expression of movement. Flowing movement was also one of the chief characteristics of the art of the Baroque period. Bernini's choice of fluid wash and chalk enabled him to create forms which flow easily into each other and into the surrounding space. The fountain, representing the interpenetration of form and surrounding space, became a popular subject for Baroque artists. This drawing, for all its spiral movement into space, is perfectly balanced about the central axis. As a sculptor, Bernini was very aware of the importance of the center of gravity. As in many Baroque works, the drapery begins to take on a life of its own. The turns and twists of the figures, the flying drapery and fins all extend into the surrounding space, making it play an active part in the sculpture.

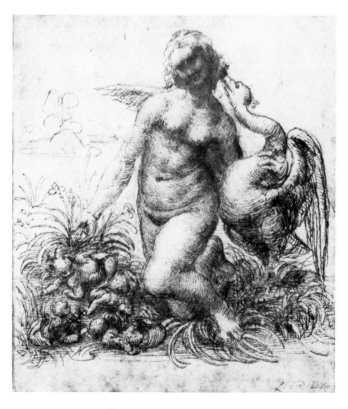

37. Leonardo da Vinci
Leda and the Swan

Leonardo da Vinci has always been regarded as one of the world's greatest draftsmen. Although he was not particularly interested in classical mythology, he was fascinated by movement and by organic growth (see Ill. 97). He made detailed studies of the human embryo which are scientific in approach, as well as this piece of poetic allegory, where babies are seen hatching from eggs. (This is one of several similar preparatory sketches Leonardo made for a painting, now lost, of the story of Leda and the swan.) Leonardo uses the freedom of chalk and wash to soften the edges of the forms (a technique known as *sfumato*). This allows them to merge imperceptibly into each other and into the background. Leonardo was left-handed, and the rounded forms are fully modeled by the use of a close hatching made up of curved lines traveling from right to left. Leda's pose is as sinuous in movement as the neck of the swan.

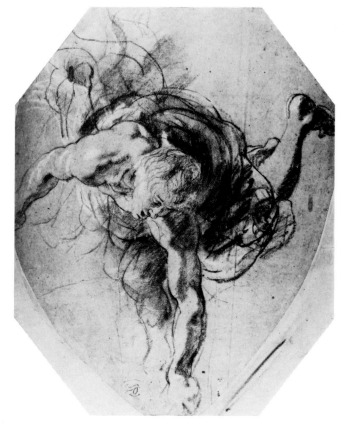

38. Peter Paul Rubens
Study of a Figure for the Descent of the Damned

One of the chief characteristics of the Baroque period was the emphasis on movement (see Ill. 36). Rubens' study of a figure in space (thought to be either Mercury or a damned soul) expresses powerfully the feeling of falling. Various successive views are apparently superimposed on each other, creating a sense of an uncoordinated confusion of arms and legs as the body twists, turns, and swoops in its headlong descent. The use of swirling drapery to crystallize the sensation of movement was another device developed during the Baroque period. Here it is used to reinforce the feeling of rotation.

39. Michelangelo
Study for a Flying Angel

Michelangelo's drawing of a man falling through space (perhaps a Fallen Angel) is a typically meticulous study of the anatomy of the male nude. This subject was of primary interest to the great sculptor. But there is little sense of falling or of weightlessness. The foreshortening and the pose generally seem to have been arrived at by observing a static figure lying on an inclined plane. The knee and the outstretched forearm would be in contact with this surface. The figure is in fact more a study of rigid perspective than of movement. Each form is paralleled by its counterpart, appropriately reduced in size to suggest distance.

40. Rembrandt
A Girl Sleeping

In making this sketch, Rembrandt was concerned with summarizing the mood and feeling of the figure. The study is therefore not only pure calligraphy, it is also a piece of careful observation. In order to capture the essentials Rembrandt worked at speed from left to right, with a fully loaded brush. As the brush moves over the rough surface it becomes starved of wash, so that a broken texture is introduced. This creates, almost accidentally, lighter tones of wash. Atmospheric depth and form are contained in each brush stroke. The weight of tone is allowed to vary from the dense black of the foreground to the lighter tones of hand and head.

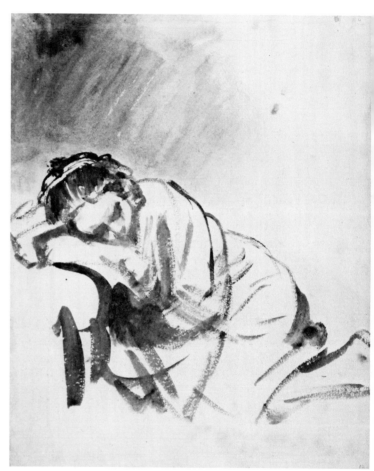

41. Henri de Toulouse-Lautrec
Woman Asleep

During his short life Toulouse-Lautrec produced some intensely personal work. He was essentially a draftsman, using line – even his paintings are virtually colored lines – as his main means of expression. His early works show an interest in animals, particularly horses. But his studies in Paris and the influence of Impressionist ideas led him to seek models from the seedier areas of life. His drawings of the *habitués* of the bars and brothels of Paris are set down with a certain detachment, though not without an ironic humor and sometimes an element of caricature. In this spontaneous sketch he has reduced the subject to its essential linear rhythms. All his drawings are concerned with movement, even when the subject is static. The fluid lines of this sleeping figure ripple over the surface, joining hair to pillow and body to bed.

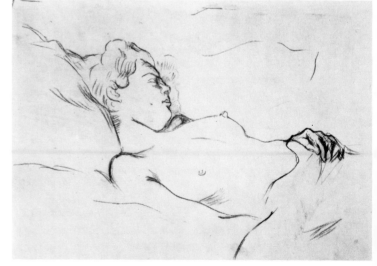

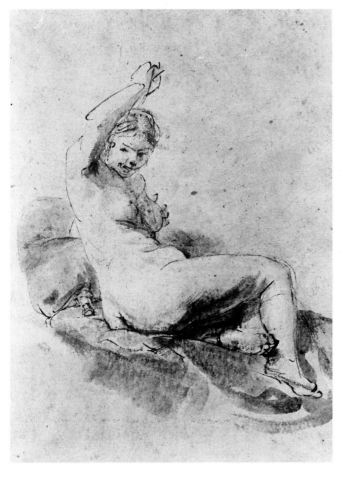

42. Rembrandt
Study of a Female Nude Reclining on a Couch

Rembrandt's technique seems to be an almost hit-or-miss affair – except that he never misses! In this pen and wash drawing the pen is used to define and punctuate the vigorous brush strokes. The ink is sometimes dragged to produce a broken texture (compare Ill. 40). Sometimes it is thinned to produce a delicate wash, giving the effect of a figure bathed in light. Light was as important to Rembrandt as to the Impressionists. For them it was the subject, the *raison d'être* of a work. To Rembrandt it represented a means of enhancing drama, emotional mood or religious content. The soft reflected lights used on the far side of the face and on the curves of the bottom contrast with the sudden sweeps of shadow on the thighs. This allows Rembrandt to capture the spontaneity of the pose – the twist of the body as the model turns to show her breasts.

43. Jean Antoine Watteau
Study for La Toilette

Among Watteau's preparatory studies are very few sketches of related groups. He preferred to draw individuals and would combine a selection of suitable subjects when he wished to produce a composition. His chosen medium was generally red chalk – the sensuous, delicate sanguine – which suited his temperament. He never used pen and ink, and rarely heightened his drawings with white, relying on the whiteness of the paper for light passages. This drawing is carried out on a pale bluish-gray paper, in red and black chalk. The red, sometimes grayed with black, is used only on the figure. The result is a delicately colored effect of warm flesh, with cool halftones, set against the silvery tones of the drapery. Positive strokes emphasize the nostrils, lips, and nipples, and combine with the soft surface modeling where the chalk is lightly rubbed. The minor axes of the head (the lines through the eyes and the mouth) and the lines of the nipples, breasts, stomach, and thigh suggest a revealing movement, like the unfolding of a fan.

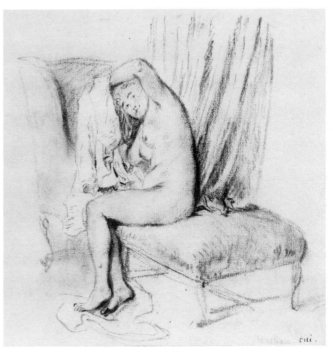

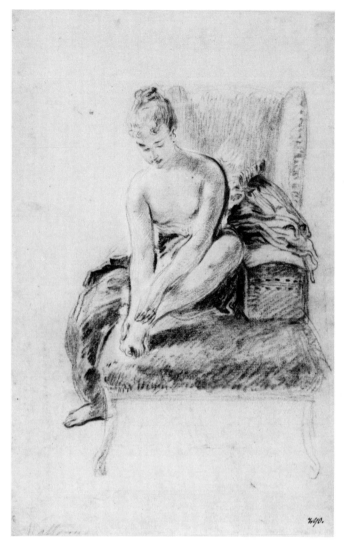

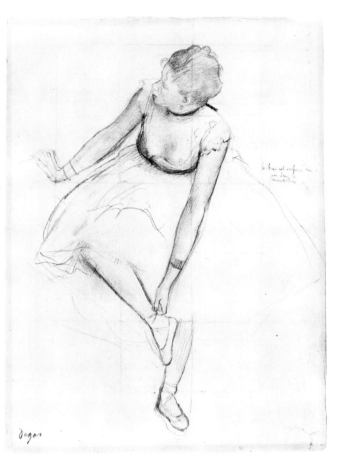

45. Edgar Degas
Dancer Adjusting Slipper

44. Jean Antoine Watteau
A Woman Performing her Toilet

Here, as in his study for *La Toilette* (Ill. 43), we see the charm and elegance of Watteau's drawing of the female form. The red chalk again tints the rosy flesh and the black chalk supplies cool halftones. Reflected lights and softly gradated shadows subtly round the limbs and create an ambiance of space, soft lighting, and mirrors.

Edgar Degas also made many drawings of women at their toilet, washing their hair, and drying their bodies after the bath. His swift, almost casual sketches suggest a candid glimpse through a keyhole. Ballet dancers and racehorses were among his favorite subjects (perhaps because both are highly trained, leggy, and professional in their movements). Degas was an excellent draftsman as we can see from this sketch, carried out in pencil and charcoal and squared up for enlargement and subsequent use in a painting. Typically, Degas has chosen a pose which emphasizes the dancer's angularity and reinforces his expression of a casual, unguarded moment. The viewpoint is, however, absolutely consistent, from the profile drawing of the head to the foot on which the body rests (and which, incidentally, describes the whole of the floor plane). The contours of the drawing are simple but firm (compare Renoir, Ill. 33). To achieve this simplicity, Degas revised and refined the contours without obliterating the original statement, so that he could estimate the degree to which alterations were required. Only very slight tone changes are needed, for example, in the arm adjusting the slipper to indicate a change of axis. The lines indicating the skirt are few, but by skillful direction and placing, the form is clearly expressed.

In 1906, at Gosol in Spain, Picasso discovered the crude Iberian sculpture which was to have a profound effect on his work. The famous *Demoiselles d' Avignon*, painted the following year, contains elements of both Iberian and Negro sculpture. It is generally accepted as representing the birth of Cubism. The figure in this drawing is treated in a similar way to the *Demoiselles* and repeats the pose adopted by one of the models. All the contour lines of this symmetrical shape are expressed in terms of convex curves, and every curve is balanced by its opposite. The V-shape between the breasts is similarly balanced by a smaller, inverted V at the base of the stomach. The only lines which do not have the curving rhythms are the hatching strokes. These are applied with a kind of crude vigor which is in keeping with the rest of the drawing. They suggest the strokes of the sculptor's chisel rather than the pen strokes of the draftsman.

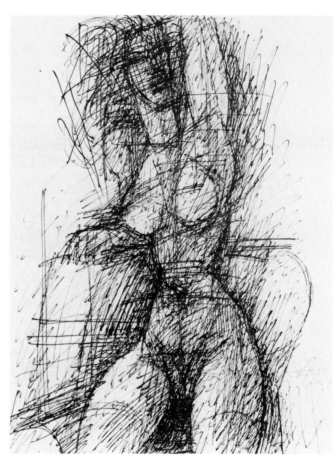

47. Marcel Gromaire
Seated Nude

This similarly stretching figure by Marcel Gromaire is drawn in pen and ink, using strong straight lines as well as curves. Gromaire once wrote that "Art is either a game or a pastime or else it is an activity, an expression for which there is no substitute." This drawing emphasizes the physical aspect of the activity. The pen reiterates the major axis, through the uplifted arm, between the breasts and through the navel to the pubic symphysis. The change of angle of the minor axes (for example the angle of the breasts compared with the angle of the hips) is also relentlessly hammered. This expressive violence is carried through into the background, so that figure and ground are joined.

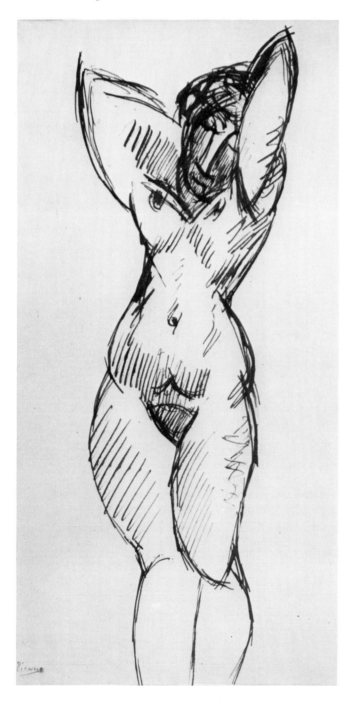

46. Pablo Picasso
Female Nude with Raised Arms

48. Gentile Bellini
A Turkish Woman

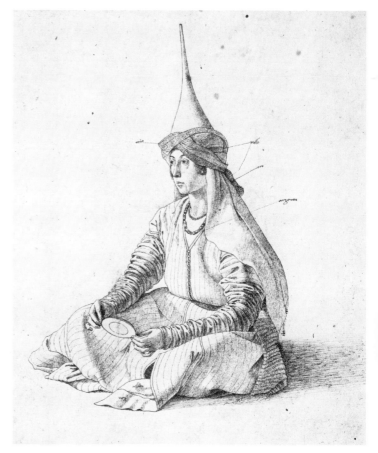

These two studies of seated figures – one by Bellini, one by Gauguin – are drawn in different media, but with a consistent viewpoint. (Gauguin's model is, of course, seen from higher up than Bellini's.) Both figures are based on the idea of a four-square block. We can visualize this more clearly if we imagine the area occupied by these seated models on a ground plan. In both cases there is a subtle *squaring up* of the lines used, in order to accentuate the idea of perspective and thereby convey the idea of forms occupying space. In Bellini's drawing of the Turk's wife this can be seen in the arms, hand, and drapery. Some of the lines appear almost ruled. In Gauguin's sketch the Breton woman's cap/forehead is a straight line, running in one axial direction. Almost at right angles to this is the line of the front edge of the cap, repeated by the twin edges of the ribbons falling behind the shoulders. Perspective is, of course, much more easily established when you can set up a relationship between two (or more) identical forms or shapes, so that parallel lines may be drawn (or imagined) connecting opposite points. The Turkish woman's knees are such parallel forms, as are the arms akimbo. Apart from the head and headdress, the perspective basis of Gauguin's study can be sensed in the rectilinear framework of the planes of the apron and even in the squared end of the sleeve. This indicates where the hand is firmly placed on the implied ground plane.

49. Paul Gauguin
Woman of Brittany

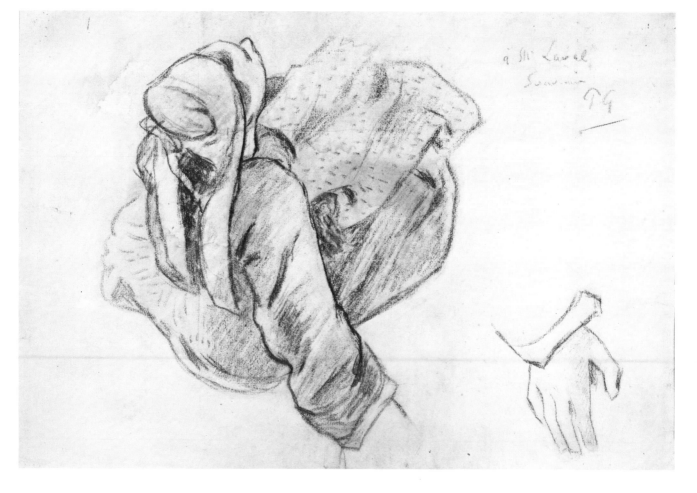

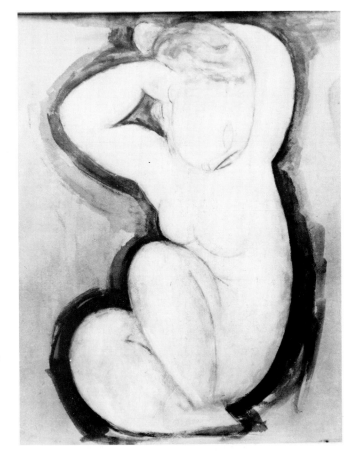

50. Guercino
Seated Nude with Arms Upraised

The ink line, varying from barely perceptible to emphatic, enriched by a wash with a similarly wide range of expression, is typical of Guercino's brilliantly inventive draftsmanship. This is not a pen drawing, nor is it a wash drawing. It is a pen-and-wash drawing resembling a duet, or, more appropriately, a *pas de deux*, where each partner complements the performance of the other. The result is a complete sense of unity.

51. Amedeo Modigliani
Caryatid

In his early works Modigliani was influenced by the drawings of Steinlen and Toulouse-Lautrec. But the Cézanne exhibition of 1907 and the meeting with the sculptor Brancusi in 1909 reaffirmed his interest in plastic form. The series of drawings of caryatids which Modigliani executed in 1914-15 represents a transition between painting and sculpture. The compact shape of this drawing – the right elbow in line with the back, the left in line with the knee – calls to mind the basis of the structure, the simple cylindrical column. The influence of Brancusi's sculpture is strongly felt in the lines of the head, which is designed to fit exactly into the enclosing arm. The features do not interrupt the simple contour. The heavy black outline/shadow serves two purposes. It throws the figure into relief and emphasizes the unity of contour configuration. Pastel is applied to the figure to round and highlight the forms.

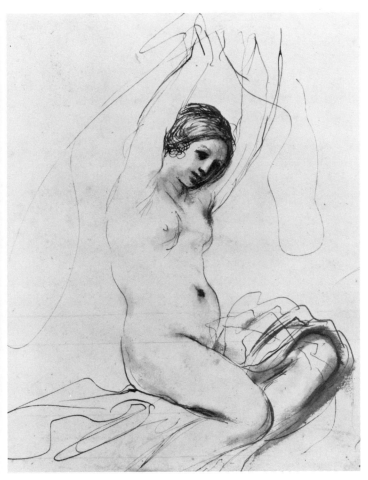

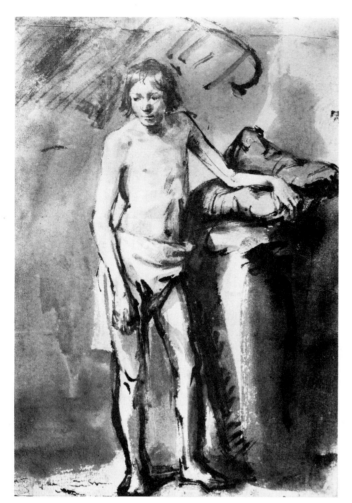

52. Rembrandt
Nude Study of Young Man Standing

Rembrandt's three-quarter view of the standing figure is carried out in bistre wash with additional pen work. The weight is taken on the model's right leg, thrusting up the pelvis on that side, so that the shoulders compensate by tilting toward us. The sense of balanced pose and the sheer naturalness of the stance, with the model's right foot well under the body to support the weight (a position always underestimated by amateur draftsmen), all add up to a subtle sense of movement. Rembrandt's hand and wash work in perfect coordination. As we often find in his drawings, the form is bathed in light, an effect created by the skillful contrast with dark shadow. Shadow is also used to convey space and depth.

53. Georges Seurat
Standing Female Model

Seurat's technique of black conté crayon on white paper (see Ill. 71) uses the weave of the paper to break up the solid black and produce a sparkle of light in shadow areas. The formality of this pose – the model looking straight ahead with the weight equally distributed on both feet, placed together – produces a static set of relationships, based on the axes of the figure. The central axis becomes a vertical line and the minor axes of the breasts and hands are at right angles to it. These directions are parallel to the edge of the paper and to the right-angled feature in the background. The vertical/horizontal structures represent Seurat's reaction to the informality of the Impressionist composition and pose (while he looks over his shoulder to Cézanne, who had also wished to restore order and structure to Impressionism). As is usual in Seurat's drawing, there are no edges defined by lines. Tones merge and edges are dissolved into background.

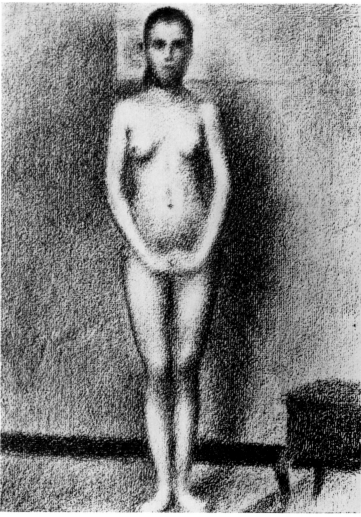

54. Henri Matisse
Nude

Here we have two different figure studies by the same artist,
Henri Matisse, one of the founders of twentieth-century art.
In 1908 Matisse wrote his *Notes d'un Peintre*. In looking at
these drawings, we can largely let the artist speak for himself.
He tells us that he dreamed of creating "an art of balance,
purity and serenity, devoid of troubling or depressing subject
matter." He summed up his aim as "simplification,
organization, expression." This simplification to pure line,
totally excluding tone, is deceptive in its apparent ease. The
more that is omitted, the more significant becomes that which
is retained. The effect of spontaneity was in fact the result of
a deliberate and painstaking subtraction. This involved a
process of gradual reduction which Matisse achieved by
tracing the significant lines of his drawing, simplifying them,
and repeating the process until he was satisfied.

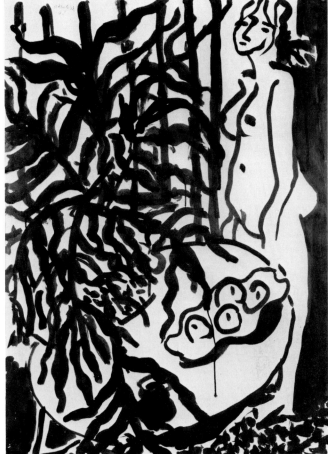

55. Henri Matisse
Nude with Fern

As early as 1911 Matisse was interested in the flat patterns
and decorative arabesques of Islamic art, with their brilliant
floral backgrounds. He experimented with them in his own
work. In this composition it is difficult to say which is
background and which is foreground since positive and
negative spaces are carefully balanced and closely integrated.
"The whole arrangement of my picture is expressive." Rarely
do we see black and white used to create such a dazzling
pattern of movement and color. It is interesting to note that
Matisse, a master of color, confined himself in all his
drawings to black and white. "A colorist makes his presence
known in even a simple charcoal drawing."

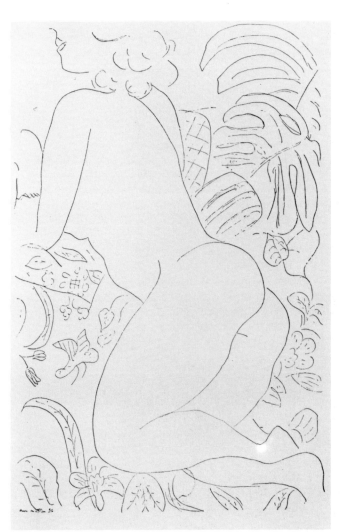

Figure Composition

Composition is the process of arranging and organizing pictorial elements within a space or area in order to produce a conceptual unity. By pictorial elements we mean the point, line, tone, and color. In figure composition these elements are simply part of or inherent in the figure(s), so that the lines of a figure may express a powerful linear thrust in a certain direction.

In designing a figure composition it is useful to have some idea of the placing of the figures on a ground plan, imagining the space required by the figures as if they were on a chessboard, and visualizing possible alternative positions. (Seurat was clearly able to do this.) Repeating units, such as heads or hands, are useful in producing a sense of rhythm or pattern. William Blake was well aware of this and often made use of it.

Linear thrusts or forces are created by lines (or implied lines, such as the direction of a gaze) moving in a certain direction. These lines are used to link together the different forms and guide the eye along predetermined visual pathways. While the linear forces are designed to produce a sense of balance within the picture space, the tonal areas of light and dark of figures or their background are largely responsible for a sense of pattern. Composition, then, is the art of juggling all these elements (and color) at once, and arriving at a feeling of unity.

The art of composition seems to have been virtually ignored by Paleolithic artists. They rarely included any representation of human figures in their work. Egyptian artists, however, developed a system of figure composition which, in spite of its rigorous limitations, proved sufficiently versatile for all their needs. Figures were allowed to overlap each other, thereby creating a certain spatial quality. Change of scale was related to social standing or degree of importance rather than distance. Since the feet of the figures were always firmly placed on the same horizontal ground line, the illusion of distance was effectively contradicted. Greek artists, judging from mosaics and ceramics, were accomplished in the art of composition. They were able to adapt their figures to fit the required shape, even when this was the circular bowl of a drinking cup. Roman artists, inheriting the Greek experience, had a basic understanding of perspective, and succeeded in arranging their figures in depth. Medieval artists concerned themselves with expressing emotional and spiritual intensity and so found the finite spatial relationships of life on earth largely irrelevant. It was only

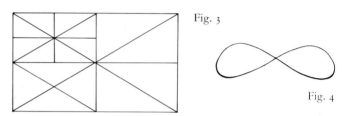

Fig. 3

Fig. 4

during the Italian Renaissance that figure composition really came into its own. Divisions of a space by its internal geometry (see Fig. 3, above) and the use of the golden section system of proportions were the guiding principles. They provided linear division, direction, and proportions for the disposition of the figures. Furthermore, with the development and increased understanding of perspective, artists were able to arrange their figures not only in depth – nearer or farther away – but also on different levels. The aim of the designer of the classical Renaissance composition was to produce a balance of shapes, forms, and forces contained within the available picture space. Wherever possible, the direction of forces and the disposition of the figures were to be parallel to the picture plane. (These principles were revived and adopted by Poussin as well as by Cézanne.)

The general effect of Renaissance composition, which is balanced and essentially static, can be symbolized by a triangle, its base firmly parallel to the front edges of the picture. Baroque composition, however, may be represented by the figure eight, lying on its side, and in perspective, describing a sense of interweaving movement in depth (see Fig. 4). The compositional attitudes of the eighteenth-century Rococo artists favored a smaller, rippling movement rather than the large sweeping waves of the Baroque artists of the previous century. In the nineteenth century the invention of the camera produced a revolution in compositional ideas. The *close-up*, where one had to look over the top of, or beyond, a foreground feature in order to see the ostensible subject, was a device borrowed from the photographer. Also derived from the photographer was the whole idea of the casually contrived *snapshot* composition, and the cutting off of edges of figures by the picture frame (see Ill. 69). But in this century it seems that some artists, for example Picasso, Matisse, and Mondrian, have preferred to return to the classical idea of a balanced system of relationships contained and confined within the picture area.

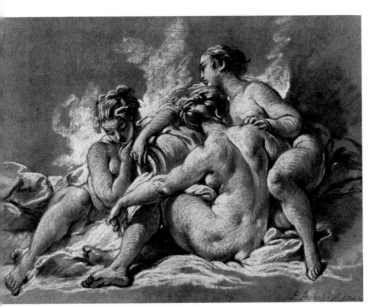

56. François Boucher
Three Nymphs

Boucher's three nubile young women seem to be the same one seen from different angles. But the view is always from a position which shows the dimples and folds of flesh to their best advantage. This tightly knit composition of intertwining arms and thighs, where all the forms (including the vessel) are fully rounded, is typical of the eighteenth-century French Rococo. This is a period which Boucher represents so well. Boucher is essentially a decorator, and his young women (like his drawings) are nothing if not decorative. His light chalk travels caressingly over the rounded forms, all of which are expressed in terms of curves. Curved lines incessantly overlap, or are overlapped, by the next. Although this may sound slightly mannered, Boucher does it with charm and elegance, and with an eroticism which is an integral part of his vision.

Boucher often uses different-colored chalks on a middle-tone paper to achieve the maximum effect of modeling. The sideways use of the chalk, chosen to create broad effects in the background, is unusual. It is a method generally shunned by artists on account of its associations with the slick or superficial approach. Boucher used it quite frequently, though, and seems to be able to get away with it quite cheerfully!

57. Paul Cézanne
Four Bathers

Cézanne's is a totally different viewpoint from that of Boucher, as we see in this rather halting drawing. Cézanne once expressed a wish to be able to "do Poussin again, from Nature." He made numerous studies for his compositions, including groups of female figures. These were not, however, always drawn from life. Following the methods of Poussin (see Ill. 79), Cézanne arranged his figures in accordance with the basic geometry of his chosen rectangle. This means that the diagonals of the rectangle (and parallel diagonals) play an important part in the disposition of major directional movements. The diagonal line of the seated figure in the foreground, continuing along the line of the outstretched arm of the standing figure, is an example of such a movement. This drawing is a formal design, based on classical principles. The figures are placed parallel to the picture plane and all are carefully arranged to create a sense of order and balance. How different from Cézanne's Impressionist contemporaries who were concerned above all with light. Here, although the light apparently comes from the left, the patches of tone appear to be quite arbitrary. In fact, they are all expressed as rectangular patches, suggesting abrupt changes of plane rather than any particular lighting effect. In short, this is a drawing of planes rather than women. Everything is conceived in terms of structure.

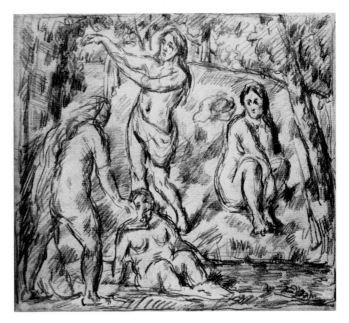

Here we see studies of the Entombment by two master draftsmen whose careers overlapped. The difference in approach is the difference between the logical and intellectual background of the Renaissance world, where everything is securely based on classical models which have stood the test of time, and that of the medieval world, where the imagination and an acute awareness of the next world is more important than the everyday reality of this one. Raphael sums up the classical art of the High Renaissance, solving all compositional problems with complete assurance. The graceful, rhythmical lines, or implied lines (such as that enclosing all the heads above the body of Christ) are contained within the picture area. Whichever linear path we follow leads to another, which in turn leads us with gentle inevitability back to our starting point. Above all, the lines are carefully balanced. The curves of the figure on the left, balanced by the figure on the right, are only the abutments for the complex balance of linear thrusts between.

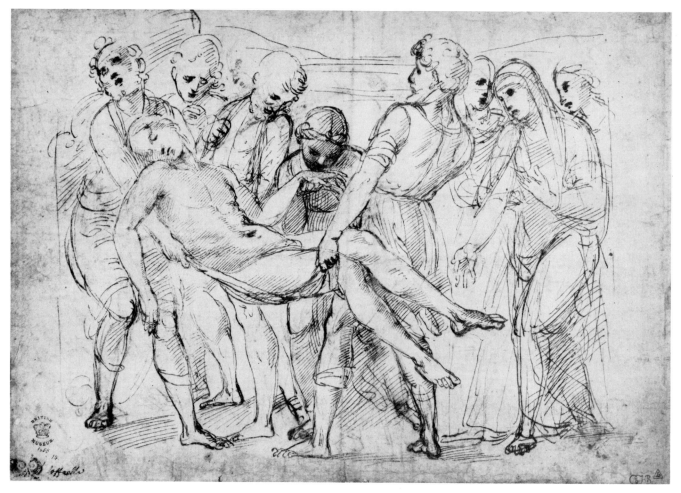

58. Raphael
Composition-Study for the Borghese Entombment

59. Hieronymus Bosch
Entombment

Bosch's version of the subject is very different in character. There is nothing here of Raphael's graceful urbanity. Everything is angular, nervous, and uncomfortable. The Crown of Thorns is upheld to show the aggressive spikes, like barbed wire. The sharply pointed beards and pointed hats, and the abrupt angularity of the drapery, all suggest pain and suffering. There is an edgy quality about the drawing due to the narrowness of tonal areas. This is in keeping with the edginess of the participants, who look guiltily over their shoulders as they are caught in the act of trying, in a kind of furtive haste, to hide the body.

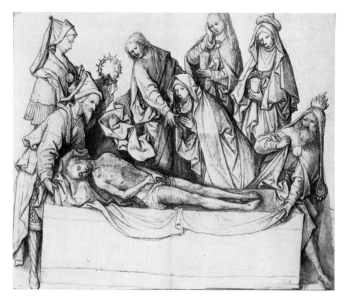

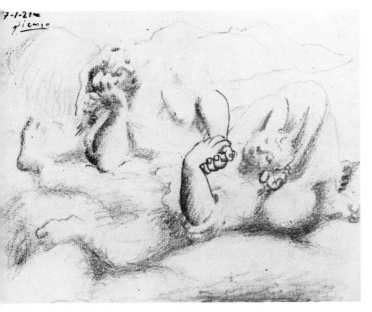

60. Pablo Picasso
Two Figures, Hands Clasped

Composition involving only two figures poses its own special problems. It is difficult to create a feeling of grouping, balance or compositional unity. The two individuals must be linked together in some way if a satisfactory visual relationship is to be achieved. Picasso solves the problem of balance by using a kind of *repeat* motif. The two figures echo each other as they adopt almost the same pose in reverse. The accentuated intertwined hands are similarly reversed and create a powerful linking device. The figures in this closely constructed composition are modeled with soft pencil on a coarse paper and are drawn in a kind of monumental sculptural idiom. This is a method to which Picasso frequently returned throughout his career. The result is a very compact unity.

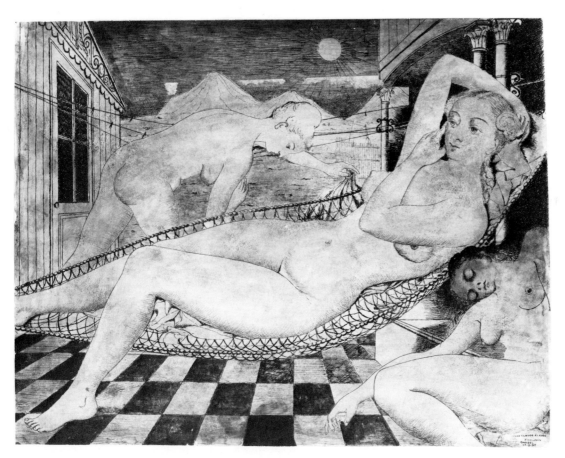

61. Paul Delvaux
The Siesta

Delvaux's composition has a similarly compact feeling. Here we have three figures, one reclining diagonally across the picture space, leaving two very awkward triangular shapes to fill. Delvaux solves the bottom right-hand corner by a particularly inventive pose. The figure in the background is related to the principal figure by a parallel movement. The central figure reclines elegantly in a hammock, whose netting construction is reminiscent of the scales of a fish. In fact the whole shape is very fish-like, suggesting a fleeting analogy with a mermaid. As is usual in all Delvaux's work the perspective is very exaggerated, the lines converging too sharply for comfort and conveying that sense of another reality which was sought by the Surrealists. Although the sun (or moon) is in the sky, there are no shadows in this dream world. What little tone there is, moves only from one side of the line to the other to give a sense of plasticity.

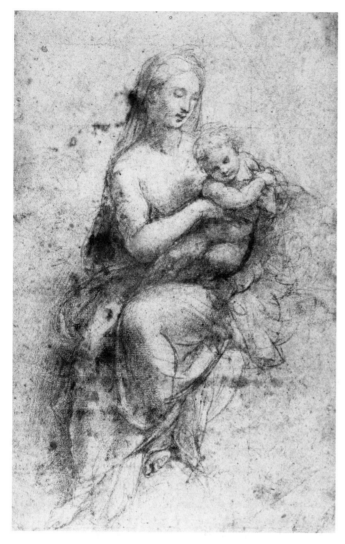

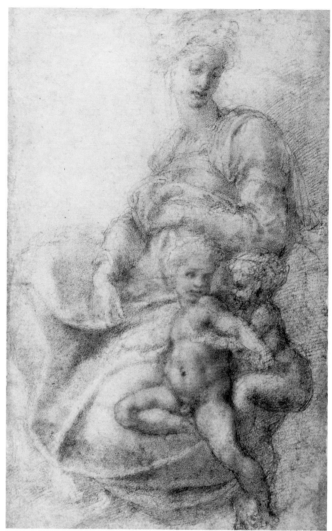

62. Raphael
The Virgin and Child: Study for the Madonna di Foligno

There are countless examples of the archetypal theme of
mother and child. Many artists of the Renaissance found it a
rewarding and challenging subject. Two figures of the same
size can present certain compositional difficulties (see Ills. 60
and 61). But in the case of the mother and child relationship,
the child can be treated as virtually part of the mother, thus
making a compact pyramidal group. In this typically balanced
composition by Raphael the main axial direction of the
Child's body is the exact counterpart of the Madonna's arm.
Raphael models his forms so that we can feel them as existing
in the logical space created to contain them. For a good
example of this quality, look at the definite distance between
the Madonna's head and that of the Child. This is an example
of the best in classical draftmanship. Form, drapery, anatomy

63. Michelangelo
The Virgin and Child with the Infant St John

of the figure, and foreshortening are all treated with an ease
and assurance based on knowledge and understanding.

The triangular grouping is almost a trademark of
Renaissance artists. Michelangelo, whose first love was
sculpture, welds the Infant Christ and St John firmly to the
Madonna. All the forms are fully modeled to suggest the
utmost plasticity. The swirling drapery forms a kind of
protective cocoon enveloping the children. Their heads are
placed to coincide with the protective arm of the Mother
Figure. Integration of individual forms into an overall unity
can hardly get any closer than in this sculptural group. So
little would have to be carved away from the original
pyramidal block!

64. Dante Gabriel Rossetti
Hamlet and Ophelia

Although these two versions of Hamlet and Ophelia are so different, the underlying *mood* is curiously similar. It has been said that one of the basic flaws of the approach of the Pre-Raphaelites was that their inspiration was literary rather than visual, and that they were preoccupied with elaborate moral allegories and images which were essentially non-pictorial. (However, Delacroix was equally inspired by literary sources without apparent detriment to his art!) This composition by Rossetti (a poet, who consequently may have tended to think in verbal images rather than in pictorial terms) is essentially claustrophobic, overwrought, and overcrowded. Not only is it overcrowded with detail, but there is little room for the figures as the spatial relationships are so ambiguous. Rossetti seems to have had difficulties with perspective. Hamlet's arm, as he plucks the rose, flourishing in the hot-house atmosphere, appears to be more a short arm than a foreshortened arm.

Everything is elaborately detailed. Surfaces are carved, embroidered or patterned. Throughout the drawing a rich interweaving pattern of lines reminds one of Celtic ornament and medieval illumination. In fact, the drawing may be read in the same way as a page from a manuscript, our eye exploring the intertwining linear rhythms.

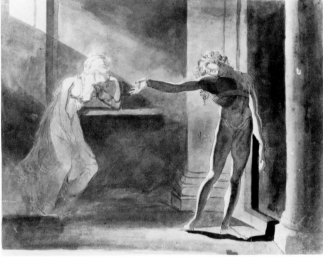

65. Henry Fuseli
Hamlet and Ophelia

Fuseli's version of the subject is very different. Instead of the overcrowded hot-house atmosphere of Rossetti's setting we have a completely bare, chillingly cold *mise en scène*, and a complete absence of detail or decoration. But there is a certain similarity of mood in both these romantic works. Fuseli's heroines, like Rossetti's, tend to drift about in trailing garments. Ophelia is shown in a state of acute ennui, bordering on collapse. (Romantic artists and poets have always tended to associate romantic love with sickness and lingering death.) Hamlet's gesture is just as languid as that of Ophelia in Rossetti's drawing. But in spite of all this dreamy posturing the drawing still makes a strong impact on us. This is largely because of its use of dramatic tonal contrast and the powerful spotlight, which creates strong shadows and illuminates the stark architectural setting, emphasizing the scene to the point where drama becomes melodrama.

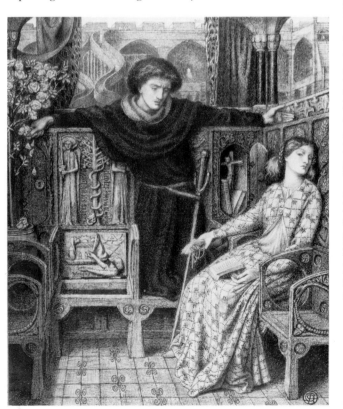

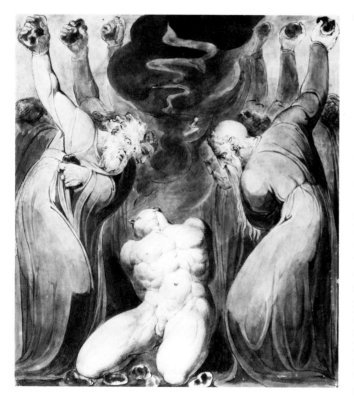

66. William Blake
The Blasphemer

"What does *precision of pencil* mean? If it does not mean outline it means nothing." The view of William Blake, poet, artist, and visionary, is reflected equally in the work of Stanley Spencer. Both artists were visionaries, seeing eternity in a flower, and taking for granted Christ on earth as an everyday experience. Blake, like Spencer, drew with clear outlines. This was partly because of his training as an engraver, but also because outlines gave the utmost clarity to his visionary experiences. These for him were more real than those perceived by the mere mortal eye. Blake's drawings can sometimes be monotonous, being based on sixteenth-century engravings after Raphael and Michelangelo. Also, as we see here, his idea of musculature is schematic rather than observed. However, the sheer power of his conviction transforms the visual clichés, enabling us to share his experiences. Such experiences, although expressed in terms of second-hand neoclassical formulas, are conveyed with a medieval sincerity and force. This composition, like many of Blake's, is essentially symmetrical. The tight handling and firm sculptural modeling derive from the compositions of Raphael and Poussin (the tradition of figure composition was not yet firmly established in Britain). The twisting rhythms of the central figure are balanced on each side by the powerful rhythms of the Old Testament figures, collective symbols of ancient authority rather than individuals. The repeating motif of the massive upraised arms suggests the repetitive movement of many, rather than just the few actually depicted.

67. Stanley Spencer
Chopping Wood in the Coal Cellar, Elsie

In Stanley Spencer's *Elsie Chopping Wood* the pencil line is almost mechanically precise. Every line is perfectly balanced (just like the archetypal figure perched on the egg box!). The modeling is slight and controlled, neat, precise, and methodical. It has nothing to do with the direction of light, but is simply an adjunct to the line. Spencer manages to give a sense of visionary significance to the mundane scene. The changing viewpoint (sometimes looking down, sometimes up), the curious, almost hallucinatory, clarity of detail, the ambiguity of space and place, the odd relationship between the three figures, and Elsie's preoccupation with something else, give this composition of taut curves a strange, otherworldly quality.

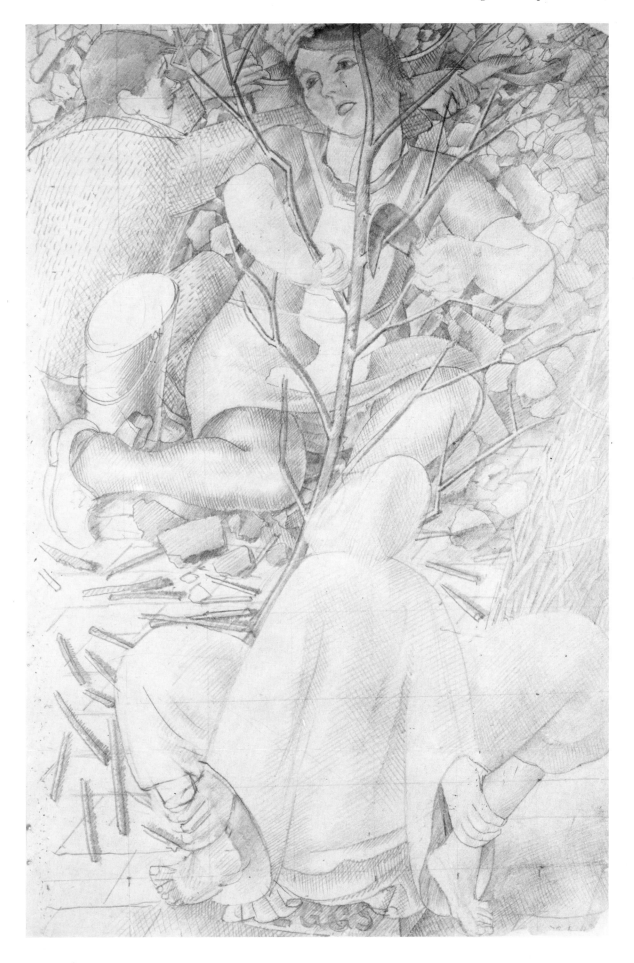

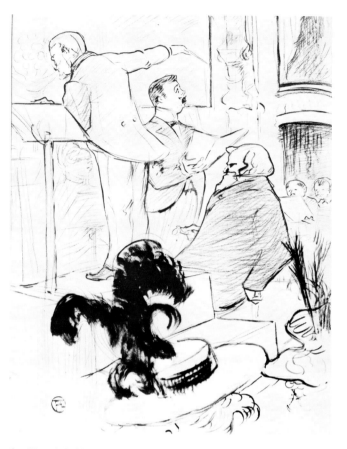

68. Rembrandt
Group of Three Women before a House

Rembrandt has built up this composition by using overlapping forms to create a movement in depth. The foreground figure is seen in three-quarter back view. The next is rotated to a near profile. The suggestion of a chair – a mere five or six lines – bridges the gap to the third figure, who is turned almost completely. Finally, the vertical edge of the counter leads us to the standing figure. She gently arrests the upward spiral and, by the downward direction of her gaze, returns us to the starting point. This is an astonishing *tour de force*. So much space and form (notice the planes of the old lady's lap, and the form of the second woman's head underlying the headdress), conveyed by so few lines – but how varied those lines are! Some are as broad and powerful as Van Gogh's. Others are delicate and gentle. But always they link up with each other, almost as if this were a piece of calligraphy in which the pen never left the page. The result is complete unity. The individuals become a group linked by a psychological awareness of each other's presence.

69. Henri de Toulouse-Lautrec
At the Opera

Toulouse-Lautrec, like Rembrandt, has built up this composition, superimposing one form on another, and using linear links to take our eye along well-defined visual pathways. Coincidental lines are used to create a continuity of surface movement. The bearded gentleman's stomach sweeps upwards to curve into the body of the singer. The tailcoat of the conductor shares the line of the music stand. But this is also a composition in depth. From the dense solid black of the magnificent plumes of the hat in the foreground, we find a gradual diminution of tonal strength as we move back in space. Although Toulouse-Lautrec's composition has much in common with Rembrandt's, there is another factor which is in evidence: the influence of the camera. The foreground opera-goers are seen in *close-up* and we must look over them to see the principal characters. This apparently casual arrangement of figures cut off by the frame is in fact very carefully contrived, and is often found in Toulouse-Lautrec's sketches and paintings.

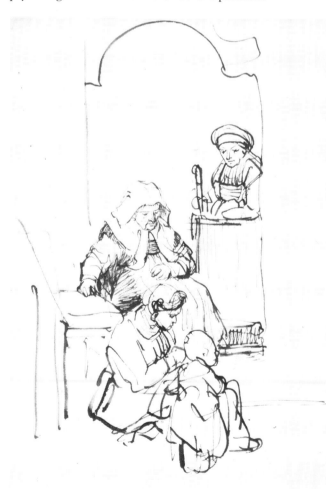

70. Thomas Gainsborough
Second Study for the Duke and Duchess of Cumberland

Here is a masterly compositional sketch by Gainsborough of the Duke and his wife strolling in the grounds of Cumberland Lodge, while the Duchess's sister sketches in the background. This is a particularly subtly balanced composition, with beautifully controlled variations in tone. In fact it is a drawing more of tonal variation than of three figures accompanied by a small dog in a park-like setting. By using stump to rub in and modify the tone, Gainsborough has produced a sense of outdoor light and shade through which the figures move. His judgment of tonal differentiation between the Duchess's hair and the background or the Duke's cravat, collar, and jacket, are examples of his perfect sense of tonal interval. Gainsborough has scrubbed in some white chalk between the Duchess's head and that of her sister as a tonal link, which completes the circular movement from the Duchess's trailing skirt and through the seated figure of her sister. In the finished painting this white patch becomes an ornamental garden urn in the background. If you half close your eyes and look at this drawing only as differences in tone, you can see that it is a balance of light and dark subtly arranged in an oval. In fact the finished canvas was painted in that format. The handling – a light, almost nonchalant scribble – produces a feathery quality which reminds us of Watteau and the French Rococo. Rococo was the inspiration for this kind of decorative work, which emphasized good manners and good breeding, and created a mood suggesting a leisurely pace of living.

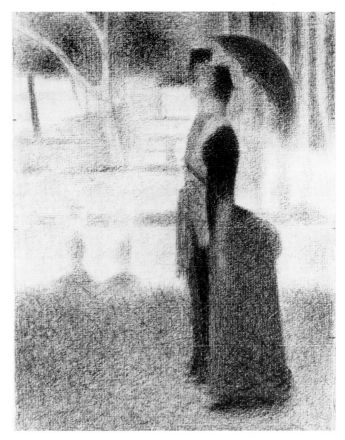

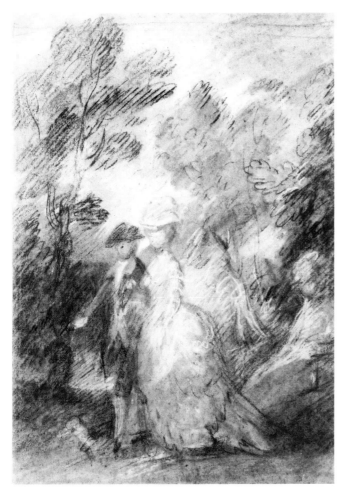

71. Georges Seurat
Study for La Grande-Jatte

Another pair of elegant figures, equally fashionably dressed and strolling in a park-like setting, form the figure study for Seurat's painting, *Sunday Afternoon on the Île de la Grande-Jatte.* The curiously stiff and formal pose of this couple is repeated in the various little groups in the final painting, giving it a strange, hieratic quality. In Seurat's preparatory drawing, line (in the sense that Ingres used it, see Ill. 34) plays virtually no part. Everything is described by tone, using black conté crayon on white paper. Seurat's application makes use of the rough texture of the paper to break up the blacks and introduce an element of light even into the darkest shadows. Paul Signac, who continued the exploration of color theory after the death of Seurat, wrote: "These are the most beautiful painter's drawings that ever existed. Thanks to Seurat's perfected mastery of values, one can say that his *black and whites* are more luminous, and even more full of color than many a painting in oils." Seurat's ability to express color through tone in his drawings was equaled only by Van Gogh's ability to express light through line.

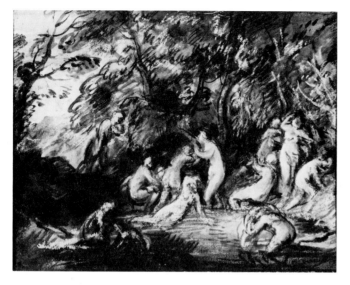

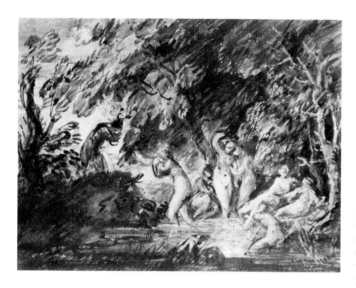

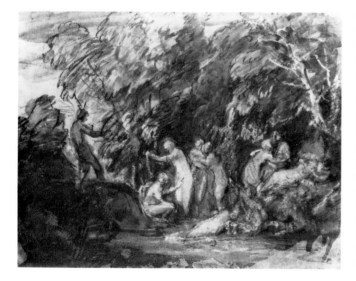

72 a, b, c Thomas Gainsborough
Diana and Actaeon: preliminary sketches

Gainsborough painted only one picture based on a theme from Classical mythology. It is also one of the very few cases where he made more than one preliminary drawing for a painting. The story relates how Actaeon, hunting in a sacred valley, accidentally discovered Diana bathing with her attendant nymphs, whereupon she threw a handful of water in his eyes and turned him into a stag, in which form the unfortunate huntsman was torn to pieces by his own hounds.

Basically, the main problem for the artist is that there are two main characters in the story, and a kind of chorus. One of the principal characters has to be separate, the other has to be part of a group. The problem, then, is how to reconcile this separation with the principles of compositional unity. The three preliminary sketches approach the subject in the same way. The semicircular pool sets the scene, and Actaeon enters abruptly from the left. In each sketch Gainsborough has kept his options open by choosing a mixed medium – chalk on wash and/or wash over chalk. By working without too precise definition he has been able to keep the composition mobile and flowing.

The first version (72a) concentrates on the idea of the confusion caused by the intrusion of Actaeon. This is expressed by treating the figures as small, separated groups, arranged along lines which recoil from Actaeon. There is a general thrust from the left towards the right-hand side. Diana's raised arm in shadow creates a rather tenuous link with the intruder. The twisted lines of trees and foliage contribute to the feeling of confusion and agitation.

In the second version (72b) Diana is moved to the left, reducing the gap between Goddess and intruder. The gap is further bridged by a much more decisive gesture. This time there are fewer figures, and the nymphs are arranged in a semicircle with Diana as center. Actaeon's forward movement links him in a definite relationship to Diana, while the nymphs become merely spectators. Tonally, this composition is much more orderly and organized. Actaeon is emphasized and singled out by being silhouetted against the light, while the silvery bodies of the Goddess and her retinue are enclosed in the curved shadow of the foliage.

In the third preparatory sketch (72c) we have Actaeon silhouetted much as before. But the general mood of the composition (Gainsborough was a master of the evocation of moods) is much less agitated than before – partly because the figures are grouped more compactly. This is the version substantially used in the *finished* painting.

In fact, the painting was never finished, in the sense of being brought to that fine degree of surface texture which is generally associated with the idea of *finish*. The final work (73) brings Diana and Actaeon even closer together. There is no need for the forceful throw to bridge this gap. Diana's gesture is much more graceful than before. She is now the center of a small, close-knit group, which is linked by the waterfall and by the movement of the figures to a subsidiary reclining group on the right. Actaeon, instead of being separated by silhouetted tone, now sinks into the shadow and becomes part of the background. He is no longer seen as a serious threat to this group of bathers – nor as a disruptive influence to the unity of Gainsborough's composition.

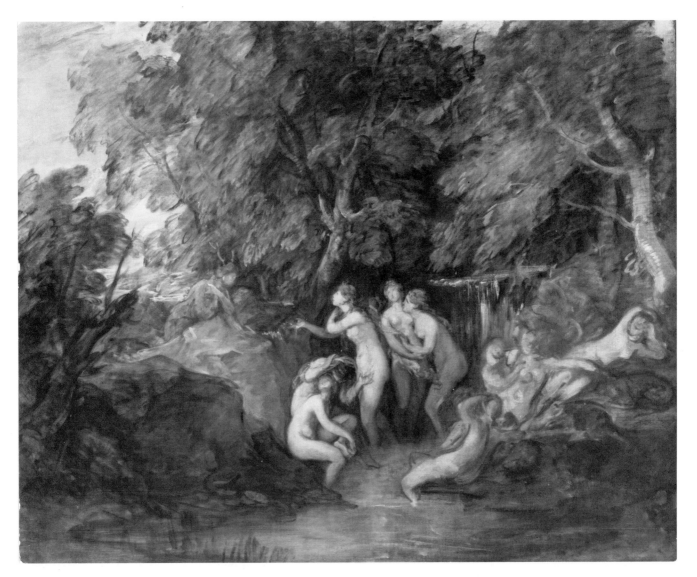

73. Thomas Gainsborough
Diana and Actaeon

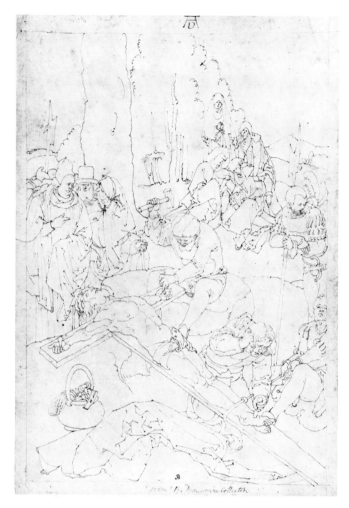

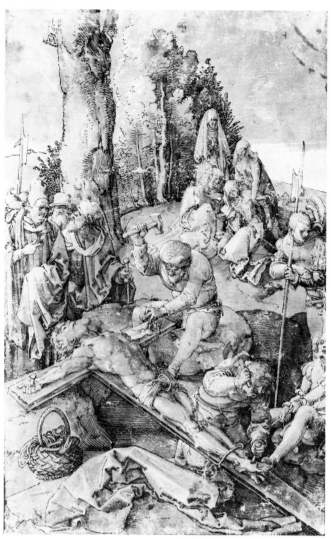

74. Albrecht Dürer
The Nailing to the Cross

These two studies by Dürer of Christ being nailed to the
Cross, one in line only, the other in tone, belong to a series of
twelve drawings of the Passion (one of which has been lost).
The linear construction of the composition, clearly defined in
the first study, consists of a diagonal leading in from the
bottom right-hand corner. This is directed back into the
picture by the top line of the Cross. This initial diagonal lead-
in leaves the problem of how to deal with a triangular space
on the bottom left. Dürer uses this space for the tools of the
trade of the workers who ply their grisly craft with all the
objective professionalism they would devote to any other job.
The carpenter's mate, bracing his foot against the Cross to
get a better pull on the rope, creates a linear movement
parallel to the top of the Cross (and to the poised hammer).
This helps create a sense of space through the use of parallels
shown as converging in perspective.

75. Albrecht Dürer
The Nailing to the Cross

In Dürer's second study the sense of depth and space is made
much more tangible by the addition of tone. We now see that
the Cross is supported on two convenient boulders. The
foreground drapery becomes almost part of the landscape.
The drapery line follows through to the shadow of the
boulder, beginning a sweeping movement which continues
behind the trees to the distant hill. The addition of tone also
makes clear the main divisions of the landscape into
foreground and middle distance. This corresponds to the
main and secondary figure groupings. The relationship
between groups of figures and groups of trees is now
revealed. Finally, the tone is responsible for the sense of
surface modeling on the forms. The tree trunk becomes
rounded with surface indentations, the anatomical details of
Christ's body are thrown into relief, and the textural
differences become apparent (on the basket, for example).

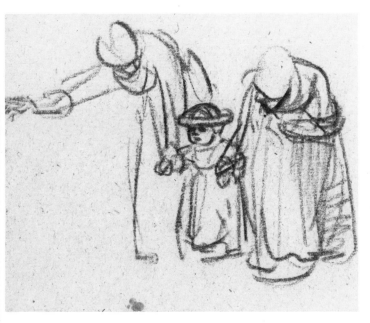

76. Rembrandt
Two Women Teaching a Child to Walk

This arrangement of three figures is one of the most expressive drawings in this anthology. The figures move diagonally across the page as our eye is led to the outstretched arm pointing to the ultimate goal. This goal is all the more difficult for us as well as for the child to reach as we do not normally read from right to left. The ground plane is not drawn at all, but is clearly implied by the perspective of the figures.

By applying less pressure Rembrandt has allowed the texture of the paper to *grin through* the chalk, breaking up the heaviness of the line where comparatively less emphasis is needed. Particularly well conveyed (with Rembrandt's usual economy of means) are the turned heads of the assisting women. Their bodies are foreshortened as they bend forward, looking toward their joint responsibility. Also, as we so often find in Rembrandt's compositions, there is a feeling of the characters' psychological involvement and awareness of each other's presence.

77. Henry Moore
Two Women Bathing a Child

While Rembrandt's drawings are those of the painter/etcher, Henry Moore's are those of the sculptor. This drawing is concerned primarily with form. The tone is applied solely with the intention of trying to express this idea. There is no attempt to use the direction or quality of the lighting to convey mood, drama, or even the time of day. This is a purely formal invention, a set of three-dimensional forms created to balance each other. When one cylindrical arm grasps the child, the balance is restored by the arm opposite which grasps the bath. To Henry Moore space is just as important as form. His close network of lines explores the spaces between as carefully as the forms themselves. It is irrelevant that the jug, bath and table do not bear any semblance to actual objects. What matters is the feeling of monumental form and the space in which that form exists. This feeling is powerfully conveyed by Moore's use of mixed media to express the cross-section of a particular form at a given point.

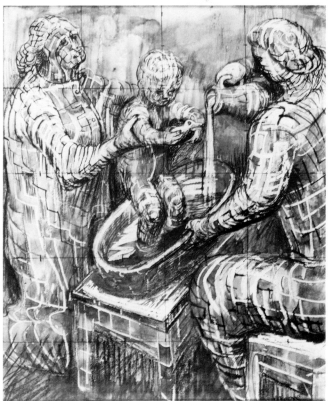

78. Vittore Carpaccio (?)
The Adoration of the Magi

This pen and wash drawing attributed to Carpaccio is another good example of a classical composition. It is similar to Poussin's study in many respects. The main group of figures is placed on a raised dais, a kind of shallow stage, which is parallel to the picture plane. As in Poussin's version, the figures are arranged in a triangle (compare Ills. 62 and 63), with the Madonna and Child on one side balanced by the three Magi on the other. These three are themselves arranged in an ascending sequence forming a triangular group. There are other triangular arrangements within the composition. (These arrangements are related to grid lines which are based on the division of the rectangle as shown on page 60.) The setting is very simple, giving the impression of being movable stage scenery. It consists of some Roman ruins and a *stable*, roughly adapted from a grandiose fragment of some unlikely architecture. The stable serves as a dark mass against which to set the figures. Carpaccio uses short broken lines to reinforce and punctuate the wash, which supplies the tone, and thereby conveys a strong sense of form. (Note that tone is not used to convey information regarding the value of colors.) Carpaccio's structural approach to the rendering of form can be seen clearly in the treatment of the subsidiary group opening the chest. In fact, all the forms are conceived initially as simple, block-like shapes.

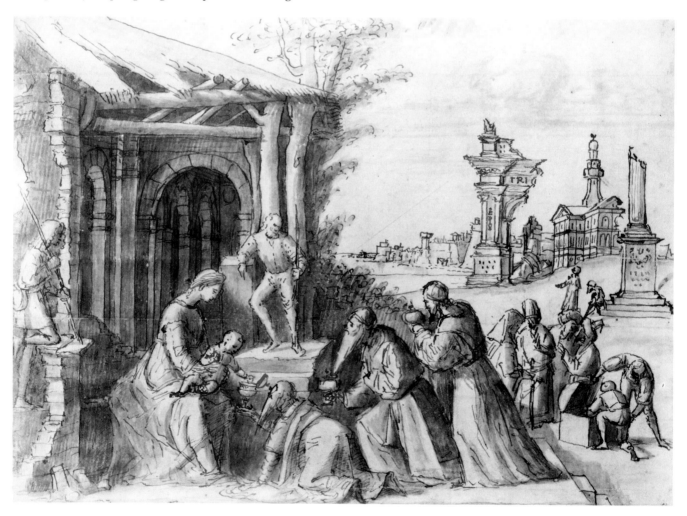

79. Nicolas Poussin
Adoration of the Magi

Poussin first went to Rome in 1624 and was enthralled by the classical antiquities which surrounded him. Thereafter he spent most of his creative life in Italy. His drawings are simple and direct in technique. He often chooses pen and wash, using the pen line with sure precision to define, and the wash to create atmosphere and form. Here there is little detail or ornamentation, little facial expression (note the anonymity of the Infant Christ), and a bare minimum of architectural setting – a wall parallel to the scene and one broken column. This is an example of a classical composition in which the whole is greater than the sum of the parts. How is it achieved? The answer is simplicity: simplicity of means plus a perfect sense of balance. Light shapes are balanced by dark.

Thrusts of gesture and pose are balanced within the space depicted. Solids are balanced by spaces between them. The *action*, as always in classical composition, takes place as if on a stage, with both stage and figures disposed parallel to the picture plane. We also sense the underlying geometric framework of the composition. This gives it that feeling of logic and formality that is typical of classical work. The drawing is divided horizontally into three equal areas. The top line, along the top of the wall, defines the horizon and links the heads on each side. The bottom line is defined by the outstretched arm which links across to the suppliant Magus.

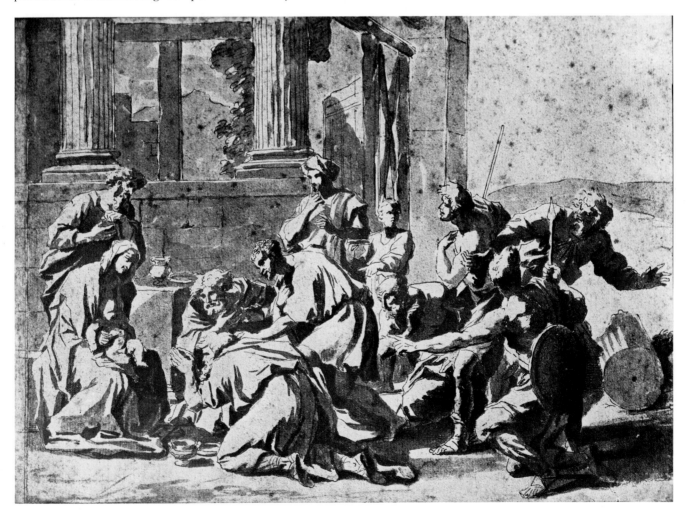

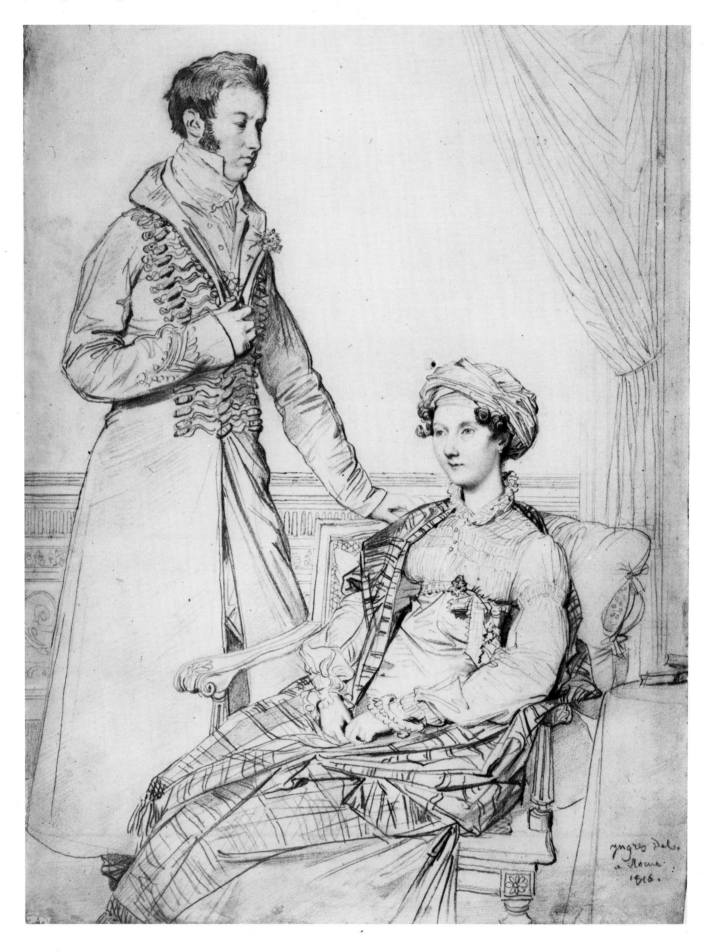

81. Pablo Picasso
Diaghilev and Selinburg

Picasso was a virtuoso draftsman and displayed his skills to their full extent in his pure line drawings. If you study the lines of the seated figure in this sketch you find that by subtle emphasis on straightness and parallelism Picasso has created that sense of perspective which is entirely responsible for the feeling of form. Tone is completely absent. The squared brim of the bowler hat describes the form of the head, while the parallel line of the lapels and the center line of the shirt tell us about the form of the body. The lines of the clasped hands are equally straightened, especially the single line where both hands overlap. This line, common to both hands, is responsible for describing the form of the lower hand. The diagonal composition of seated and standing figures is given compositional unity by linking the figures together with coincidental lines. The hat joins the sleeve and the sleeve joins the lapel.

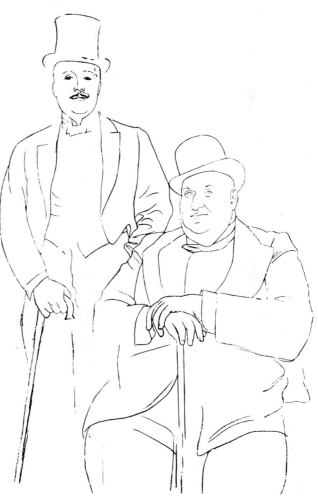

80. Jean Auguste Ingres
Sir John Hay and his Sister, Mary

In Ingres' drawing we see once again the clear yet subtle line of Raphael. This double portrait is an example of sheer observation and accuracy of detail expressed through masterly control of the medium. (The extreme sensitivity of Ingres' technique would not have been possible without the invention by Conté in 1795 of the new form of graphite pencil encased in wood.) Ingres believed that line itself should suggest *la forme intérieure* with the minimum of modeling. Tone is therefore used very sparingly on both the forms and the background, and only lightly indicates on which side of the line it exists. The variation in the strength of pencil line suggests depth. The drapery in the background, for instance, is only lightly delineated. The patterned drapery across the shoulder of the lady is strongly drawn compared to the adjacent hand and chair. Farther back still the wood paneled dado is only faintly drawn. As in Picasso's drawing of Diaghilev and Selinburg, the diagonal composition is carefully arranged to give a balanced relationship to the two figures. The arm resting on the back of the chair provides a physical link between the two individuals and the downward glance of Sir John reinforces the effect of bridging the gap.

Landscape

The popularity of landscape as a subject for painting has varied considerably throughout the history of Western art. The Egyptians sometimes suggested landscape as a symbolic setting for figures. Greek and Roman artists considered it a subject in its own right. During the Middle Ages landscape declined in importance, eventually re-emerging as the Enchanted Garden (Eden or Paradise) of the manuscript illuminators. But it was the Flemish artists of the fifteenth century who were the first to establish the subject. This fact was recognized by Michelangelo (whose own concept of the Garden of Eden consisted of a single tree). He wrote of the Flemish painters, "Their painting is of stuff, bricks and mortar, the grass of the fields, the shadows of trees and bridges and rivers which they call landscape, and little figures here and there. And all this although it may appear good to some eyes, is in truth done without reason, without symmetry or proportion, without care in selecting or rejecting." Michelangelo's contempt for landscape as a trivial subject would not, however, have been shared by his great contemporary, Leonardo, whose scientific curiosity extended to the depiction of scenery.

In fact, some of the greatest artists in history have been intrigued by the peculiar and particular problems of landscape painting. One major problem is the physical difficulty of working out of doors (although this was an approach rarely used or even considered appropriate until Constable and the Impressionists). Then again, there is the sheer scale of the subject. There might be a vast distance to be expressed. This is a problem not always successfully solved. It generally involves creating a continuous sense of space from foreground through middle distance to background, without abrupt transitions — a technique which baffled many early masters of the Renaissance. Another great problem is that caused by the ceaseless movement and constant change of Nature. Constable said that the best lesson in art that he had ever had was "... that light and shadow never stand still." The changing light and shade and the shifting panorama of clouds are more noticeable in the British Isles (and the Low Countries) than in Mediterranean lands. It is therefore not so surprising that a great school of watercolor drawing should have grown up in Britain. Taking an example from Claude and working outdoors, Constable and Turner produced on-the-spot watercolor drawings[1] of the most fleeting effects of nature. "Light – dews – breezes – bloom – and freshness yet not one of which has been perfected on the canvas of any painter in the world." Although this was Constable's view, it seems in fact that these evanescent qualities were well expressed both by himself and by Turner (whose later work was described by conservative academicians as "paintings of nothing and very like").

Watercolor is the ideal medium for capturing those varied and variable effects, the *chiaroscuro of nature* that go to make up the weather of Britain's cloudy islands. The transparent, fluid character of watercolor enables washes to be delicately floated over others. This creates effects of light, dews, breezes, and blooms, while retaining a quality of freshness and vitality. Another advantage to the landscape painter is the portability of this medium. This greatly aided Turner as he traveled and sketched through mountains, storms and rains, hail, steam and speed.

---

[1]Watercolors are referred to as drawings since that was what they were originally called. Often they depended on pen or pencil for reinforcement or clarification. In fact the pointed sable brushes used for this work were called *pencils*. The word is still used by some painters and decorators to describe this kind of brush.

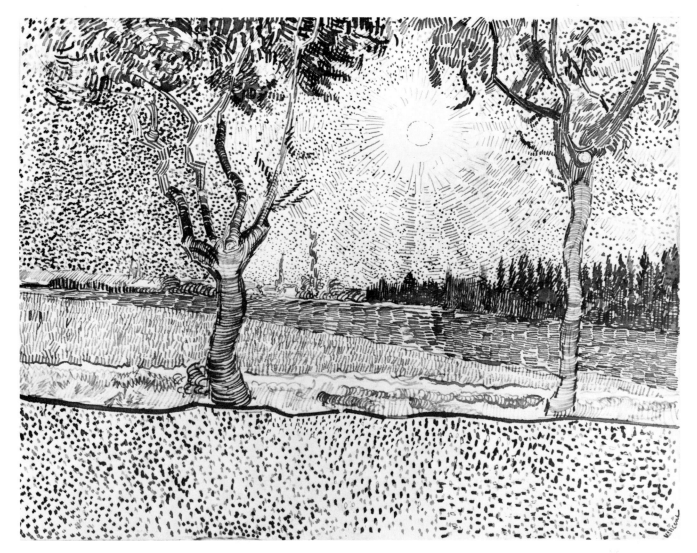

82. Vincent Van Gogh
The Road from Tarascon

83. Samuel Palmer
Landscape

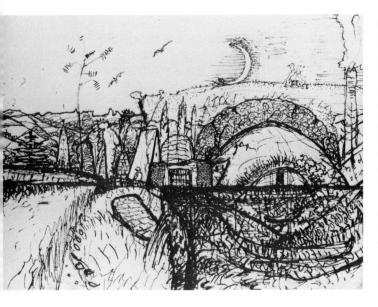

Van Gogh's pen and ink, as in all his work, is ablaze with light, yet strangely enough there are no cast shadows. He uses a very personal technique involving short, straight pen strokes (curved for the curved forms of tree trunks), defining different surfaces by appropriate treatments. The close pattern of moving points conveys the tone and color of the sky. The sun, dazzling in its brilliance, makes it impossible to see anything in its proximity. A different, more open texture of points, still imbued with movement, is used to describe the road. It is separated from the edge by the only continuous line in the drawing.

We proceed from sunlight to moonlight. Samuel Palmer's landscape shows the same absence of shadow as Van Gogh's drawing, but a very different mood. Palmer was inspired in his early work by a meeting with William Blake, whose vision of the world of the imagination was more real to him than the everyday world. In this romantic drawing, Palmer's shapes, though clearly defined, are as difficult to name as in a dream. Shapes (Are they trees? Boulders? Buildings?) curiously related by a similarity not only of shape but of texture, overlap, yet without much sensation of depth. Through a crumbling bridge (?) we seem to see another (or an eye?) on the same horizon line. The moon, balancing on edge, echoes the bridge shape and birds wheel in the sky. The landscape is transformed by imagination into a different world.

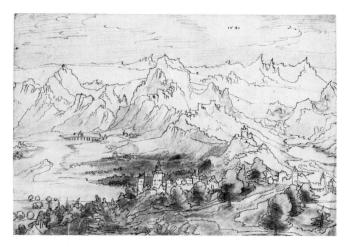

84. Wolfgang Huber
Mountainous Landscape with a Fortified City

OPPOSITE:
86. John Constable
Tillington Church

Wolfgang Huber was a German painter and graphic artist noted mainly for his woodcuts. Signs of his skill as an etcher are evident in the way he carefully outlines all his forms with pen and ink before applying thin washes of limited color. This sketch shows the romantic approach to landscapes. This is a landscape of mood, fantasy, and fairy tale. The mountain peaks, crowned by suggestions of buildings, overlap each other in a continuous sequence. Roelandt Savery presents us with another Alpine landscape, equally romantic. Indeed Savery's drawings, although executed considerably later, have many of the characteristics of Huber: the same preoccupation with edges, and the same brittle forms overlapping each other without much feeling of depth. The fantastic rock formations remind us of those in Patinir's paintings, and the background to Leonardo's *Virgin of the Rocks*. Like Huber, Savery was also known for his graphic work. We can see in the essentially linear character of his drawing the same needle sharp, hard, and uncompromising qualities as in his etched line. The shattered pine tree with its spiky branches is reminiscent of the turrets and towers of the period.

John Constable is often considered the father of modern landscape. Before Constable, *landskip* painting had been dominated by the notion of the picturesque, producing scenes which were intended to remind the spectator of a picture. These were done generally by Claude. Constable worked on his sketches outdoors, mostly in his native Suffolk. Although he states that they describe scenes he saw on the banks of the River Stour, he had also studied carefully the compositional method of Claude. Constable developed his own method of working which was to make first a small oil sketch direct from nature, backing it up with pencil sketches. He would then make a full scale sketch in oils before embarking on the finished work. His preliminary pencil sketches, sometimes (as here) with added transparent washes of color, have a shimmering vitality which he found difficult to maintain throughout the process of producing his finished works. His large oil paintings, exhibited at the Royal Academy, were nevertheless widely acclaimed. Although this is a very small sketch (approximately 10 in. × 9 in.), it has the breadth and sweep of a much larger picture. It exemplifies the *dews, breezes, bloom and freshness* which Constable sought to capture.

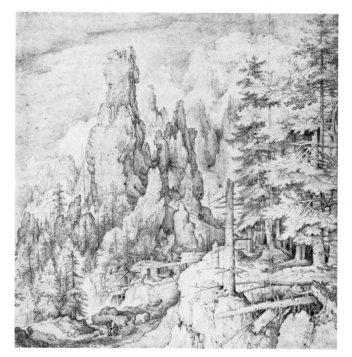

OPPOSITE:
87. Thomas Gainsborough
Cart on a Woodland Road

Thomas Gainsborough, too, found inspiration in the Suffolk countryside. Although equally proficient in portraiture and landscape, he once expressed the view that he would like nothing better than to abandon portraiture, take his viola da gamba (he was something of a musician), and paint landscapes. In this wash drawing, using a brush fully loaded with wet color and limiting his palette to two or three colors at most, he has produced a splendid play of sunlight and an effective massing of light and shade. There is something in the handling – a kind of scribbling, feathery treatment of the foliage – which recalls the technique of Fragonard. It reminds us that this is the eighteenth century, the age of elegant decoration and the Rococo.

85. Roelandt Savery
Alpine Landscape

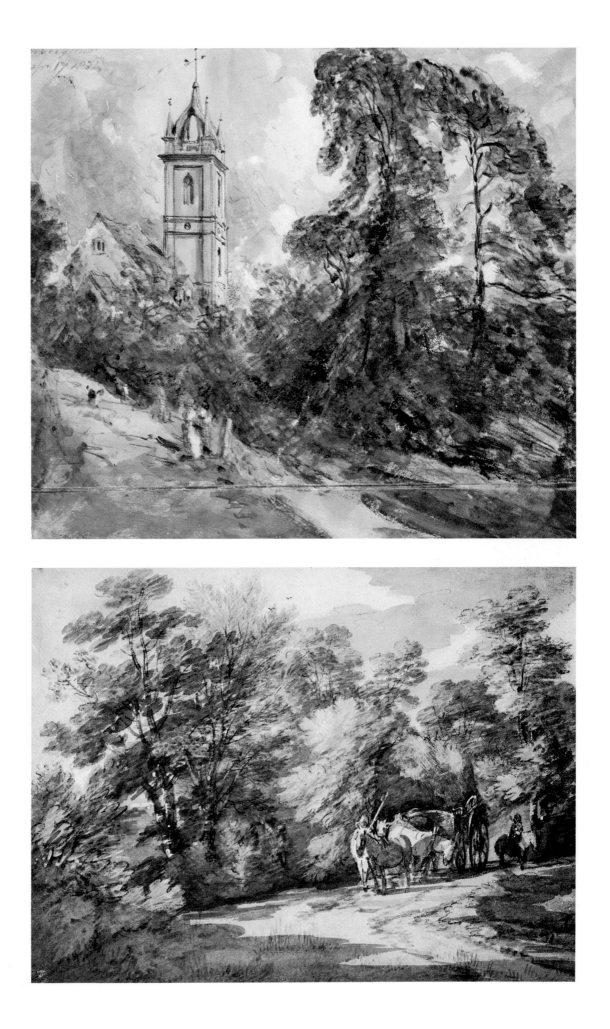

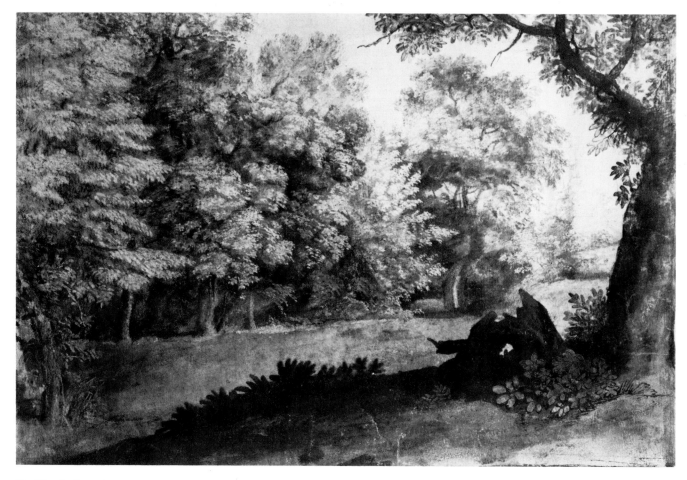

88. Claude Lorrain
Clearing in a Wood near Rome

Claude Lorrain, although a French painter, lived and worked in Italy. He had considerable influence on landscape painting (and landscape gardening). In fact the idea of the *picturesque* was largely associated with Claude's composition. In this drawing Claude brings the diagonal foreground of his drawing forward by emphasizing the tone of the shadow and by reversing the use of warm color for this area (the diagonal lead-in to the picture was a favorite device of Claude's). The near tree and the bank on which it stands are used as a kind of dark frame for the more distant wood. The expression "you cannot see the forest for the trees," meaning that the whole is overlooked due to preoccupation with detail, is quite inapplicable in this case. The silvery masses of foliage remain resolutely masses and the leafy details suggested are kept subordinate to the forms.

89. Adam Elsheimer
River Landscape

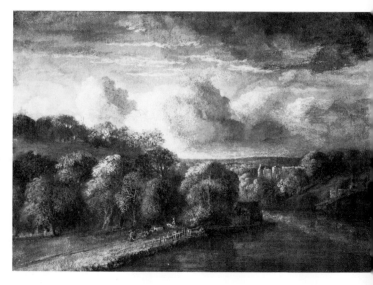

Using a very limited palette, one warm color and one cool color, Elsheimer has achieved a very convincing sense of distance and form. He divides the picture to give us more sky than land. This is unusual, since sky is often arbitrarily dismissed by many landscape artists. But Elsheimer makes both sky and land of equal interest. It seems almost as if the trees (of similar rounded shape to the clouds and lighted from the same direction) are reflected in the sky but in reverse – the larger tree opposite the smaller cloud and vice versa. The lightest part of the sky comes against the darkest part of the wood. Similarly, the distant light on the far bank of the river, as it bends out of view, is emphasized by the contrast with the dark foliage of the trees on the near side of the river. This throws the woods into relief and helps bring the near bank forward.

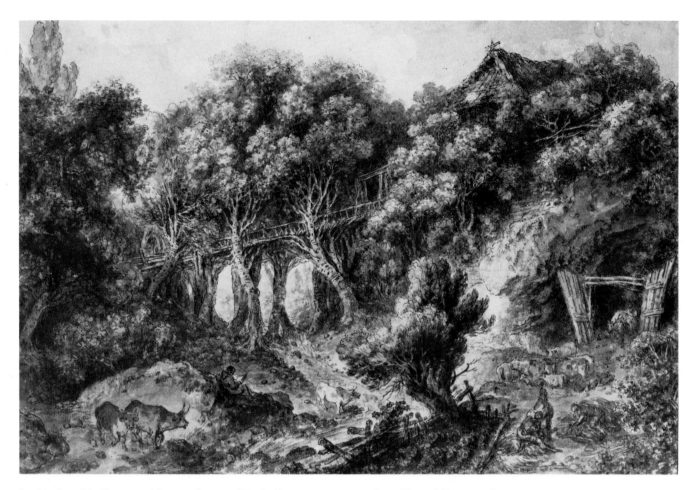

90. Jean Honoré Fragonard
Landscape with a Bridge through Trees

In this drawing Fragonard has made use of basically two colors, a cool blue-gray and a warm sepia. The warmer, stronger tones are reserved for the foreground and cooler, lighter tones for the background. This produces a vaporous atmospheric effect and a treatment of space typical of Rococo art. The feathery treatment of the foliage and the graceful curves of the tree trunks are also in the best vein of the Rococo. However, the muted colors and general air of decay produce an atmosphere of subdued sadness. The drawing is very skillfully composed and is constructed in such a way that shapes are drawn by a continual counterchange of light against dark tones. The cattle are silhouetted against the light side of the foreground rock. On the dark side of the rock the figure is silhouetted against a light passage. Follow the contours of the foreground tree and notice how the background always becomes lighter when the tree is darker, and vice versa.

Dufy, who exhibited with the Fauves in 1906 and who was once a successful textile designer, is sometimes dismissed as a mere decorator. The spirit of his work suggests a kind of twentieth-century Rococo. In fact Dufy once compared himself to Fragonard. In his drawing he developed a kind of deceptively casual, sketchy, and spontaneous style. But this kind of throwaway treatment is not as easy as it looks (as his many imitators, seduced by his nonchalance and charm, have found). Dufy's drawings are a brilliant improvisation, a kind of visual shorthand. Foliage is summed up as one rounded brush stroke, punctuated by the black inverted commas of leaves, deftly flicked in.

91. Raoul Dufy
Olive Trees by the Golfe Juan

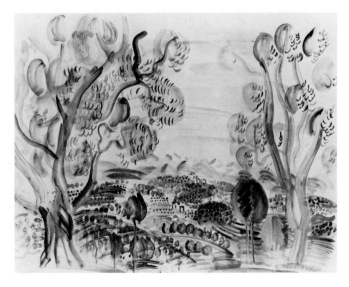

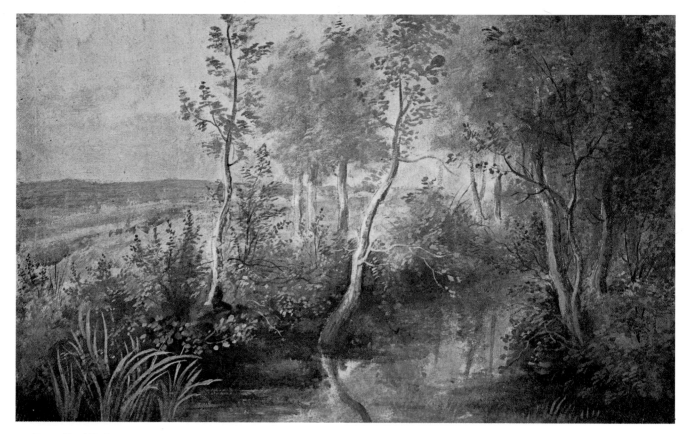

92. Peter Paul Rubens
Trees Reflected in Water at Sunset

It is difficult to equate this quiet scene of a small stream
overhung by trees with other works by Rubens. He is noted
as the supreme master of the Northern Baroque. With his
brilliant team of assistants he expressed the triumph of the
Counter-Reformation in vast, spectacular painting. In 1635
Sir Peter Paul Rubens (he had been knighted by Charles I
while on a diplomatic mission to London in 1629) bought a
country residence, the Castle of Steen. During the last five
years of his life, when not fulfilling commissions, he painted
landscapes for his own satisfaction – and, in this intimate
study of lush growth on the water's edge, for ours.

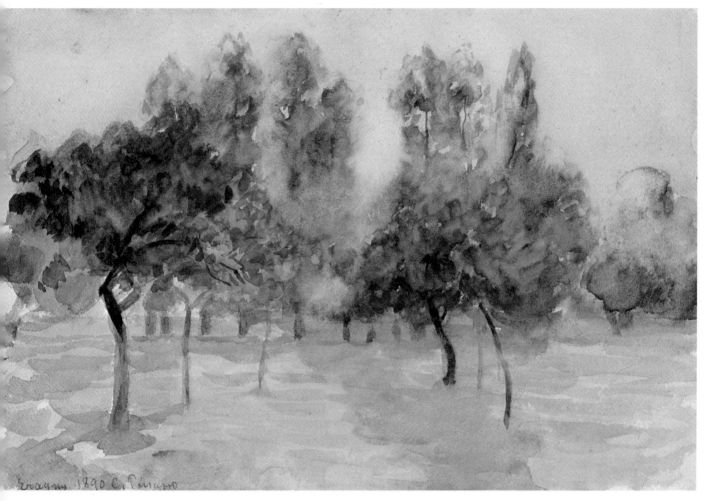

93. Camille Pissarro
An Orchard

The freshness and the complete lack of stylistic overtones
make this drawing as *modern* today as it was when it was
painted. There is little one could say about Pissarro's
watercolor study of an orchard at Eragny (where he settled in
1884) that would not be equally applicable to Rubens' sketch.
Both have a freedom and spontaneity of handling which
imbue the pictures with a feeling of light and fresh air.

Cézanne's drawings cannot be appreciated or even understood without some knowledge both of his aims and of his work as a whole. Cézanne was *not* trying to reproduce the appearance of a scene (or anything else) in paint. Instead, he strove to find visual equivalents to "realize his sensations." Unlike the Impressionists, who were concerned to record the effect of light on a particular scene on a particular date at a particular moment, Cézanne concerned himself with what he called "the geological substructure" of nature. By this he meant the formal relationship of the composition and its internal rhythms. All Cézanne's drawings show a painstaking analysis of structure expressed in terms of planes. Foliage, rocks, and tree trunks are all unified by being seen as structural forms. Cézanne ignores accidental effects of light, atmospheric perspective, fleeting shadows, and textural differences in his determination to concentrate on the solid and durable.

Mondrian takes Cézanne's analysis even further. The colors, textures, leaves, and branches of his apple tree are reduced to basic linear relationships. The proportions and rhythms found within the tree's structure have themselves become the subject of the drawing. The trunk has been reduced to a central vertical axis, around which the branches are indicated by analogous curves. These are related to a vertical/horizontal system which provides a sense of structure and foreshadows a fundamental element of Neoplasticism – the relationship of the vertical and horizontal. Tone in this drawing has nothing to do with indicating light and shade, or creating the illusion of form or imitating the appearance of the tree in any way. It is used simply to provide a slight sense of depth, of partial relief, while preserving the essentially two-dimensional nature of the paper on which the drawing has been created.

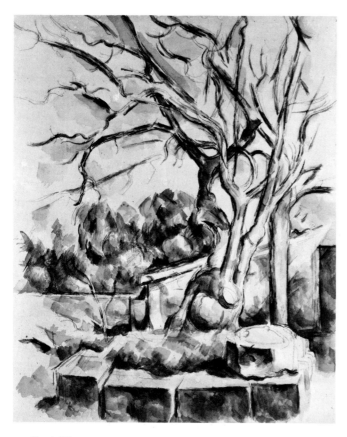

94. Paul Cézanne
Pistachio Tree at Château Noir

95. Piet Mondrian
Apple Tree

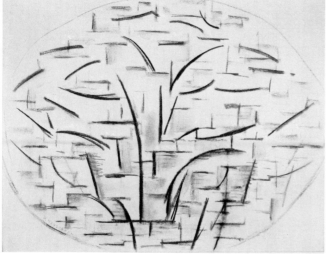

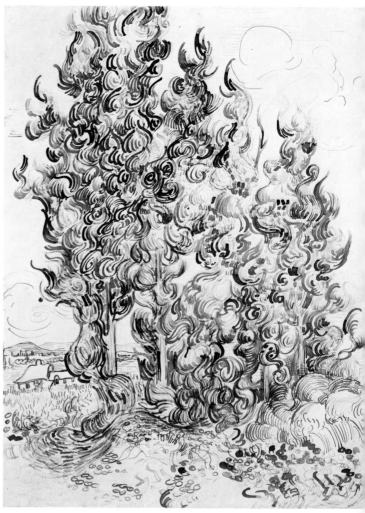

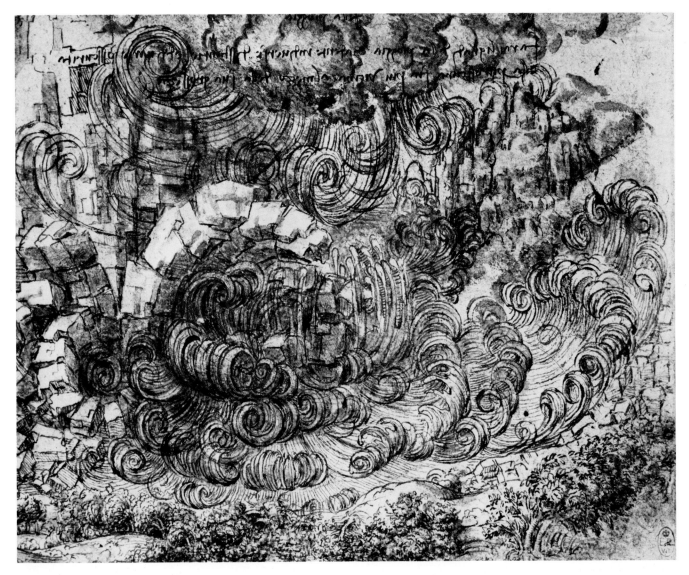

96. Vincent Van Gogh
Grove of Cypresses

97. Leonardo da Vinci
A Deluge

Van Gogh's cypresses convey the same kind of energy as Leonardo's deluge (although in his case *frenetic* might be a more appropriate description). All his drawings express movement and disturbance, reflecting the emotional disturbance of the troubled genius. Van Gogh developed a very personal, graphic style of drawing. He used a reed pen to produce dots and dashes (almost a kind of musical notation), swirls, and spirals, all in continuous but controlled movement. Everything Van Gogh painted – the sea, the distant rolling hills, even the background of a portrait – whirls and eddies like smoke.

From the asylum at St Rémy on June 25, 1889, Vincent wrote to his brother: "The cypresses are always occupying my thoughts. I should like to make something of them like the canvasses of the sunflowers, because I am astonished that they have not yet been done as I see them. They are as beautiful in line and proportion as an Egyptian obelisk."

What has Leonardo, the very epitome of the intellectual approach to art of the Renaissance, and who took so long to complete so few paintings, in common with Van Gogh, pouring out his feelings in paint and producing most of his paintings in only two years? In his relentless pursuit of knowledge, Leonardo made studies of movement in all fields, including the flow, currents, and eddies of water, and the force exerted by its continuous movement. "The water which you touch in a river," he wrote, "is the last of that which has passed, the first of that which is to come." This apocalyptic drawing of the forces inherent in movement is one of a series which shows the power of Nature unloosed. It depicts Man and his world overwhelmed in crushing, grinding tumult. This pessimistic vision of human destiny, so out of keeping with the Renaissance view of Man as the measure of all things, reminds us uncomfortably of the terrifying force of Nature. The swirling spiral lines of this drawing are a powerful expression of irresistible force and kinetic energy.

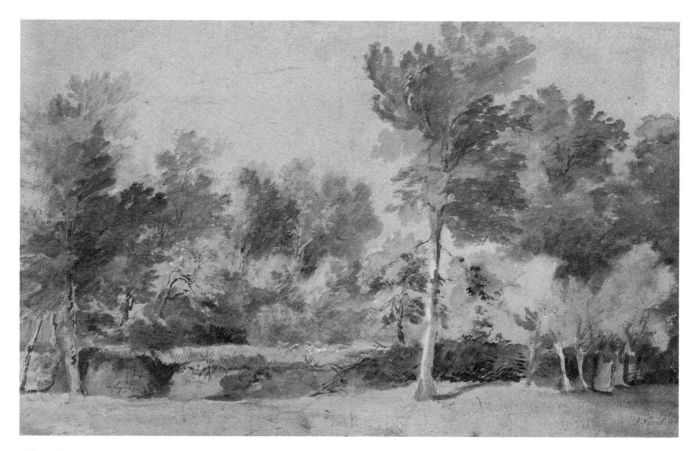

98. Anthony Van Dyck
A Meadow Bordered by Trees

Van Dyck's watercolor drawing is carried out with an elegance and skill which befit Rubens' most brilliant pupil. But it is in an idiom quite unlike the Grand Manner of the Baroque. The blue-gray color of the paper, with slight modification, is responsible for the sky. It is in fact used as a moderating influence on all the other colors. The result is a quiet harmony and unity of mood which gives the drawing something of the quality of a tapestry carried out in closely related colors. The trees are simply drawn as a balanced combination of flat, silhouetted shapes and more three-dimensional forms. Van Dyck is here exploiting the technique whereby forms may be originated as apparently three-dimensional and the continuation of the form may be treated quite flatly, even silhouetted. By association the flat will appear as an extension and part of the solid.

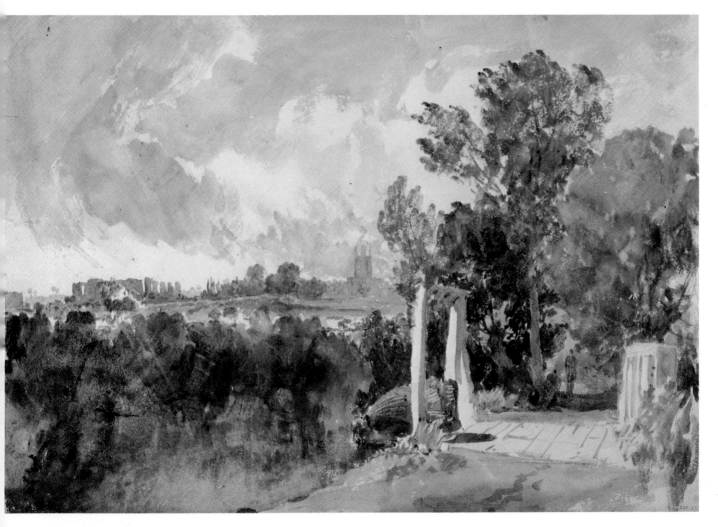

99. J. M. W. Turner
Benson or Bensington, near Wallingford

Like Van Dyck, Turner often used a blue paper as the support for his sketches, particularly those in body color. He has chosen white paper for this watercolor, however. Turner has taken full advantage of the transparency of the medium which he found so suitable for expressing watery reflections merging into each other, the changing mood of the sky, and the shifting shadows of foliage. Turner was an incomparable master of this difficult medium. He was submitting competent drawings to the Royal Academy at the age of fifteen, and throughout his life watercolor remained his favorite medium. The translucent wash effect of his later oil paintings (described as "pictures of nothing, and very like") reflects the experience he had gained from the transparent medium of watercolor. Throughout his career Turner became increasingly absorbed with light and color. The ostensible subject of his work gradually disappeared, dissolved in a blaze of colored light or lost in a mother-of-pearl mist. The light in this drawing comes from the skillful use of the white ground, which illuminates the sky and provides the sparkle on the surfaces of leaves and water.

100. Vincent Van Gogh
La Crau from Montmajour

Here we compare two pen and ink drawings of extensive panoramas, both seen from raised viewpoints. In Van Gogh's drawing the movement follows a kind of zigzag route along road, rail, and hedge, into the far distance. The surfaces of the fields are all activated by small strokes of the pen, creating myriad moving points. The sense of space and distance in this drawing is chiefly the result of the difference in scale of the pen marks, which become closer together and more compact, as well as smaller, as they recede. As in all Van Gogh's drawings, the whole seems to be full of light as well as life.

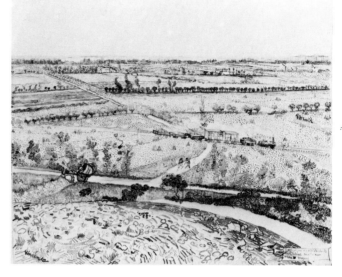

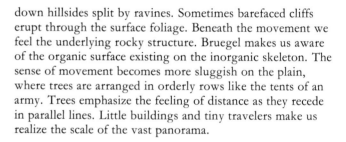

101. Pieter Bruegel
Alpine Landscape

Bruegel, too, uses many small-scale marks in his pen drawings of landscapes. He varies both the strength and scale of the marks according to the distance. In the foreground of this drawing – part of the high, rocky escarpment from which the scene has been observed – the marks consist of dark, continuous lines expressing a kind of flowing movement. In the distance the marks become fainter and more broken. But the sense of flowing movement runs through the whole drawing. The trees, like boiling froth on molten lava, flow down hillsides split by ravines. Sometimes barefaced cliffs erupt through the surface foliage. Beneath the movement we feel the underlying rocky structure. Bruegel makes us aware of the organic surface existing on the inorganic skeleton. The sense of movement becomes more sluggish on the plain, where trees are arranged in orderly rows like the tents of an army. Trees emphasize the feeling of distance as they recede in parallel lines. Little buildings and tiny travelers make us realize the scale of the vast panorama.

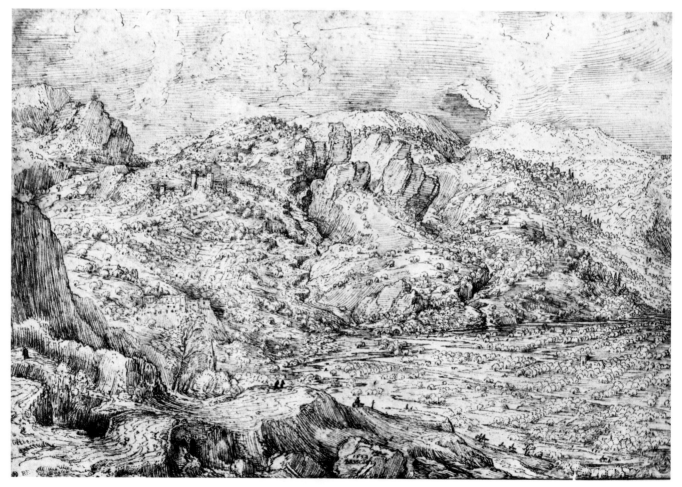

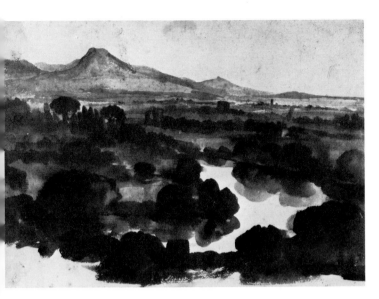

102. Claude Lorrain
The Tiber above Rome: Evening Effect

By the simplest means, a series of beautifully controlled washes, Claude produces a landscape with a true sense of recession. We experience this recession in terms of precise intervals of tone, enabling us to progress into the distance by a series of orderly steps. As one step is silhouetted against the next the lower edge is softened, creating the impression of an evening mist rising from the low-lying ground. By contrast, against the dark foreground, the light sky reflected in the river is dazzling. All Claude's drawings (however simple) and paintings are imbued with a sense of light (compare Van Gogh's *La Crau from Montmajour, Ill. 100*).

103. Georges Seurat
Landscape Study for La Grande-Jatte

Seurat, like Claude, was preoccupied with light. His drawings are always carried out solely in tone. He preferred the dry medium of conté rather than the wet wash. Though equally skillful as Claude in the control of his chosen medium, Seurat gradates the tones and makes his edges indefinable as they merge into each other. This produces a sensation of light dissolving the edges of the forms. This study is the background on which he will place the figures for his large composition, *Sunday Afternoon on the Île de la Grande-Jatte* (see also Ill. 71).

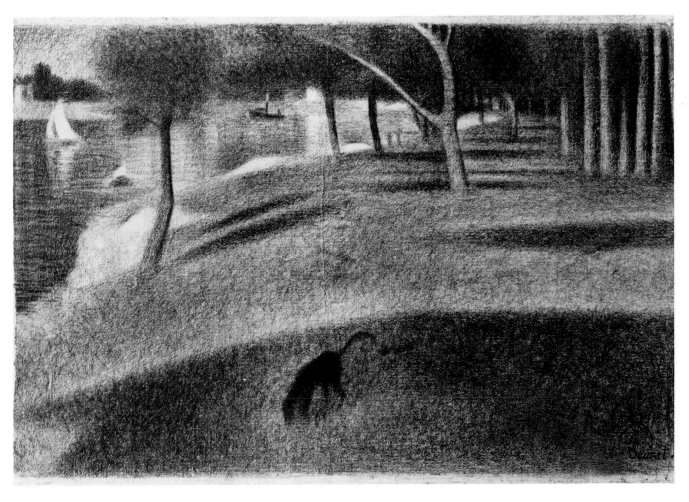

104. J. M. W. Turner
Venice, S. Giorgio from the Dogana

Turner, unlike his great contemporary, Constable, made many sketching tours throughout Europe. He found particular inspiration for his compositions in the Swiss Alps. His first visit to Italy in 1819 had a profound effect on his painting. In Rome, in just three months, he made 1,500 drawings and watercolors, though it was the romantic atmosphere of Venice that made the greatest impression on him. Turner's response to the city's charm is evident from this watercolor.

Here, the light reflected on the water, the serenity of the muted colors, and the simplicity of tone all combine to produce a mood of quiet introspection. (Surprisingly, many of Turner's works are quite the opposite in mood. Like all Romantics he had a predilection for violent thunderstorms, avalanches, fires, tempests, and shipwrecks – preferably all at the same time!)

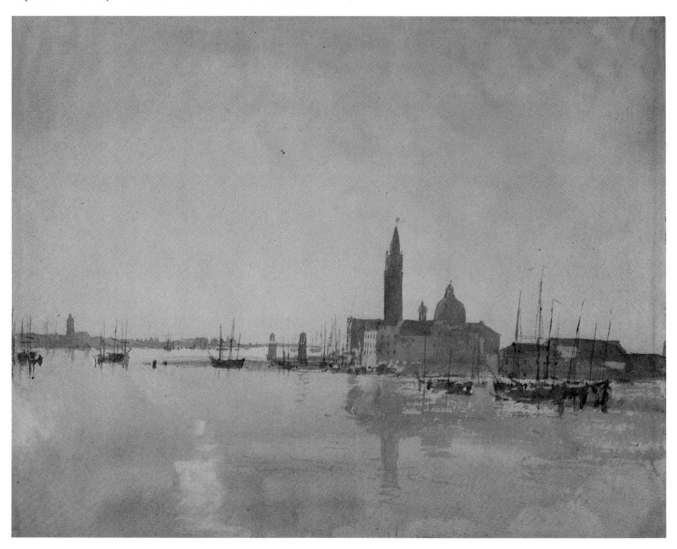

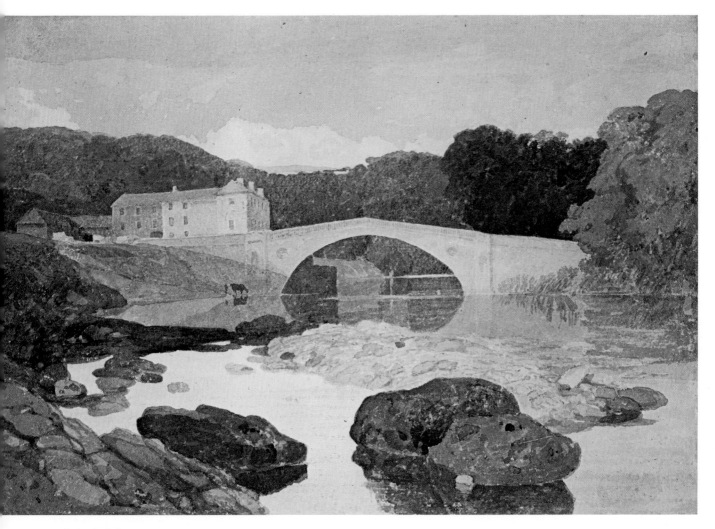

105. John Sell Cotman
Greta Bridge

Cotman, a contemporary of Turner, produced many
outstanding watercolors and oil paintings of the English
landscape. The quality of his watercolors in particular has
never been surpassed (see Ills. 121 and 122). Cotman
developed a highly original technique of silhouetting and
simplifying the form into large masses, using the tonal values
of these broad areas of color to make a strong pattern of
shapes. The masterly suppression of detail, and the power of
construction, would have been appreciated by Cézanne.

106. Alexander Cozens

A Rocky Landscape

"To sketch is to transfer ideas from the mind to the paper . . . to blot is to make varied spots . . . producing accidental forms . . . from which ideas are presented to the mind . . . To sketch is to delineate ideas: blotting suggests them . . ." So Alexander Cozens wrote in his book, *A New Method of Assisting the Invention in Drawing Original Compositions of Landscape*, published in 1785. He called the method *blotting*, and recommended putting blots on paper and using them as the starting point of an imaginary landscape. It was Leonardo's writings that had suggested the idea to Cozens. "You should look at certain walls stained with damp," Leonardo advised, "or at stones of uneven color. If you have to invent some backgrounds you will be able to see in these the likeness of divine landscapes, adorned with mountain, ruins, rocks, woods, great plains, hills and valleys in great variety . . ." But the blots or stains are only a starting point, a stimulus to the imagination. Whether or not a work of art results from this depends on whose imagination is stimulated.

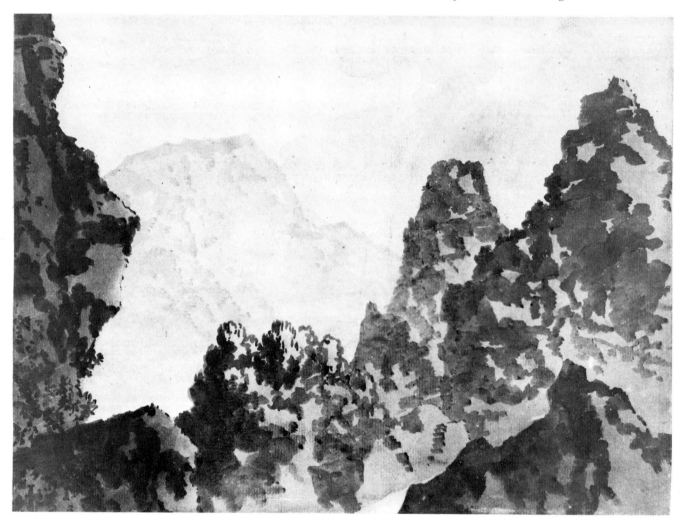

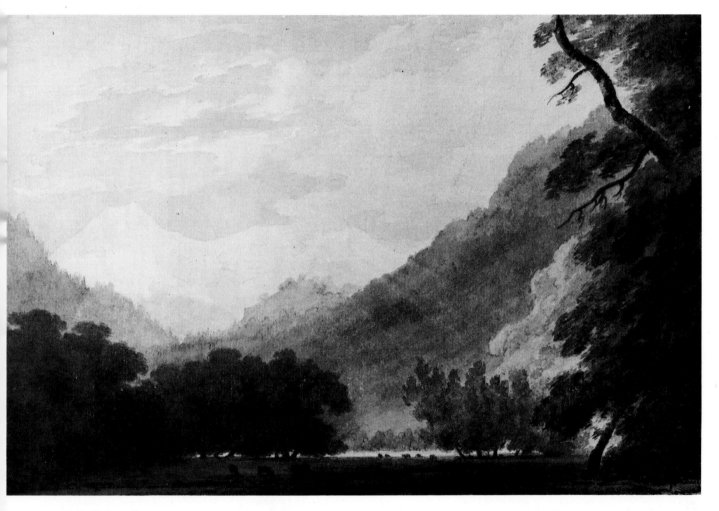

107. John Robert Cozens
Interlaken: the Peaks of the Jungfrau Group in the Distance

John Robert Cozens, son and pupil of Alexander, drew and painted Alpine scenery from the Romantic viewpoint rather than the topographical. Like his father, he used a very limited range of tone. But, as we see here, he produced very spacious effects, with a tremendous sense of scale. This imaginary rocky landscape, based on blots, is constructed on three planes of recession: foreground, middle distance, and distance. The drawing is carried out in a very limited range of tones with the darker values in the foreground, only two or three middle tones in the middle distance, and virtually only one middle tone to describe the distance. This gradual narrowing of the scale of tone is responsible for the sense of distance and atmospheric perspective.

The Built Environment

The chapter titles of this book may suggest that the pictures in each section can be fitted into neat categories. This is clearly not the case, and there is inevitably a good deal of overlap and ambiguity. For the purpose of this chapter we may take the title of The Built Environment to include any drawings in which a building or buildings play a fairly prominent part. However, we must recognize that a good deal of what we call landscape was equally *built,* and that building may very well be seen as part of the landscape, since without land you cannot build.

Throughout history artists have shown a predilection for drawing certain kinds of buildings. The noble Greco-Roman temples and arches provided a subject or setting for the artists of the Renaissance or for those favoring a neoclassical approach. To the Romantics it was the idea of ruins, crumbling or overgrown, which inspired. Churches and cathedrals (including the ruins of the neolithic cathedral of Stonehenge) have also proved a very popular motif. Others have chosen the theatrical setting. This gives full range to the artist's imagination, and allows him to invent his own built environment, expressing grandeur, fantasy or Gothic horror. The industrial landscape, on the other hand, has not proved a very popular subject. The cityscape of housing and streets is also comparatively rare. (The Futurists' love affair with speeding traffic and high-rise blocks was very short-lived.) The street scene has usually been a setting for figures. The same applies to interiors, drawings inside bars, cafés, theaters, or houses, all of which are more often backgrounds for the inhabitants than subjects in their own right.

Perhaps to the amateur draftsman the particular difficulties associated with drawing buildings derive from the problems of perspective. Here, because more straight lines are involved, the effects of linear perspective may be more evident than in a drawing of some other subject. However, a trained artist would be very unlikely to think of this as a difficulty. He would probably welcome the opportunity to explore perspective for his own particular ends.

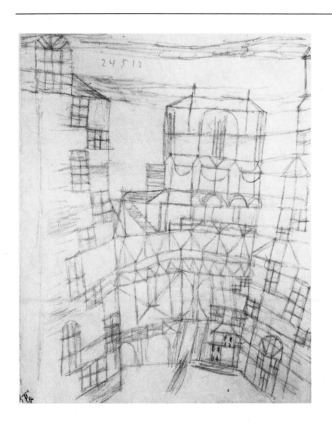

Canaletto's early training was in his father's profession of scenography. Even this drawing of a little loggia has a curiously theatrical air, suggesting a temporary construction in a light-weight material. The effect is largely due to the absence of light and shade, which are normally added to give a feeling of mass. The drawing is made virtually in oblique perspective. The *orthogonals*, parallel lines moving away from the spectator, do not noticeably converge. Had they done so the degree of distortion, because of the height of the building, would have made it look very odd. Canaletto was a first-rate topographical draftsman. His meticulous studies were sometimes made with the help of the camera obscura, though many were drawn on the spot.

This is another theatrical drawing for the same tall, narrow stage, but this time more of a fantasy. Klee's pencil sketch, apparently drawn from a viewpoint halfway up the tall building, is, like all his works, an invention and an exploration of means. In this case, Klee explores the ability of line to express space. The concept of buildings is quite incidental. They are simply a convenient peg to hang the line on. Having created a linear framework to express the idea of space in an enclosed area, Klee subdivides the framework according to a logical system based on the simple geometric division of the rectangles he has created. The result: a world of his own.

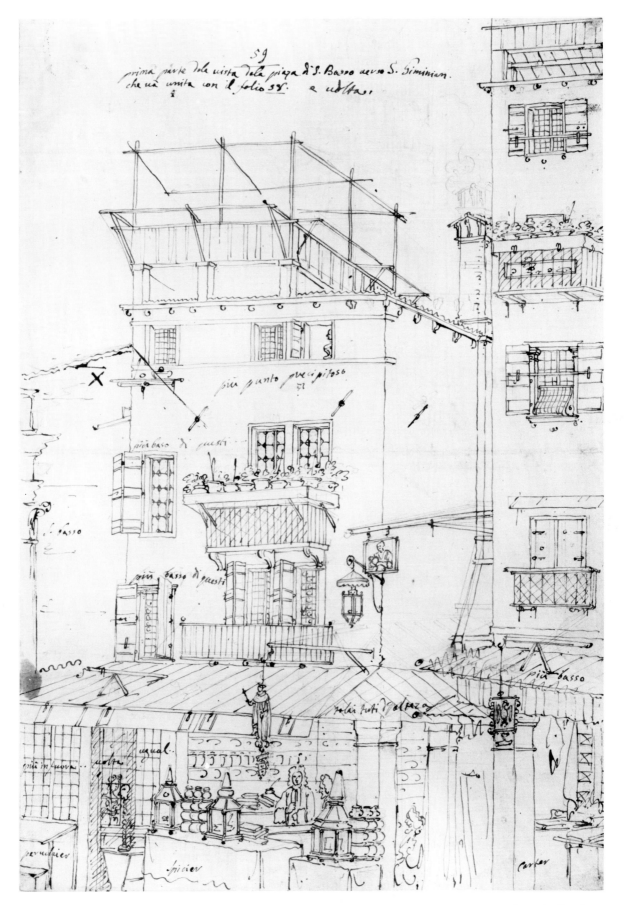

108. Paul Klee
From an Old Town

109. Antonio Canaletto
Piazza di S. Basso

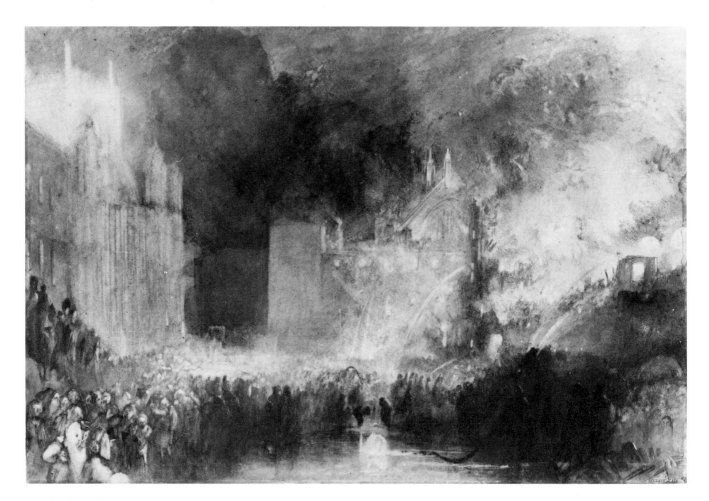

110. J. M. W. Turner
The Burning of the Houses of Parliament

We can see from this drawing why some French critics of Turner's day dismissed his work as "formless exaggeration," and his handling of color as "pyrotechnics" or "confectionery." Today we might tend to judge his imaginative treatment of color more in the context of Abstract Expressionism. Admitted to the Royal Academy Schools at the age of fourteen, Turner studied to be a topographical draftsman. (There was a steady demand for views of historic buildings at this time.) As his career progressed, however, he became more and more interested in light and color. He applied his discoveries both in oil paintings and in watercolors (in fact making little distinction between the two). A reckless technician, he scraped, scratched, or used any means whatsoever to get the effect he required. Here he used just a few colors. While the paint was still wet, he very effectively wiped it out with a rag or sponge. The subject – flames, smoke, and drama – was made for Turner. This was the one occasion where it is known that he worked directly from the subject in color. In his haste to record the apocalyptic event he blotted the pages of his sketchbook against each other.

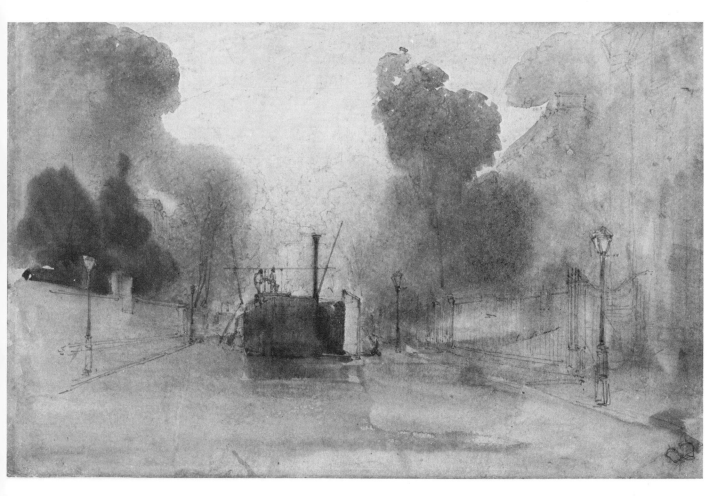

111. James Abbott McNeill Whistler
Street Scene, with Tar Engine

Whistler's approach to art, like Turner's, has much in common with that of the abstract artist of today. He spoke of treating the picture as simply "an arrangement of line, form and color." Certainly in this drawing little remains of the so-called subject. Instead of a street scene with tar engine we see space and movement. This is an Impressionist drawing, reminiscent of Monet's studies of railway engines dissolved by light and steam. Whistler, like his fellow Impressionists, was a great admirer of the Japanese print. When we look at this drawing with its evocative spontaneity, its exploitation of the wet medium so that shapes flow into each other apparently accidentally, and its feeling of flawless positioning, we can see that the influence of the East was highly beneficial to Whistler's development as an artist.

112. John Constable
The Ruins of Cowdray Castle, Interior

Here are two Masters' drawings of castles nostalgically
hinting at past glory by the light streaming through the
broken windows. The ruins of Cowdray Castle form an
unusual composition for Constable. In his work the sky is
often the major item. Here the crumbling walls tower above
us, but we can still glimpse the sky through the great
windows. What is characteristic of Constable's work, though,
is the vitality of handling, the brushwork, and the sense of
structure underlying even apparently accidental effects. The
diagonal walls are paralleled by the diagonal undergrowth in
a muted, sad green complementing the faded pink-grays of
the building. The great diagonal shadow across the far wall
heightens the effect, producing a scene of drama and
foreboding as powerful as anything in *Macbeth*.

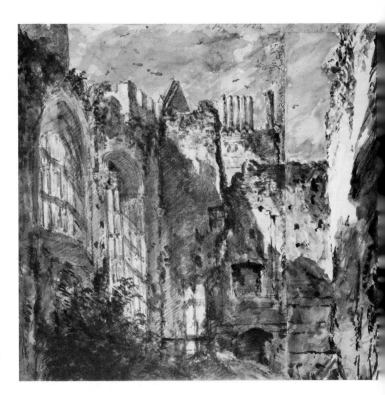

113. Thomas Girtin
Great Hall, Conway Castle

Girtin, born in the same year as Turner, died at the early age
of 27. He was one of the team of artists who met at the house
of Dr Thomas Monro, a London physician and patron of the
arts. Turner and Cotman were also members of his *academy*,
and worked at night copying Alexander Cozens and other
watercolorists. Girtin quickly developed an original style,
using a series of small, broken touches which punctuate the
main masses. This gives the whole a sense of detail and
delicacy which is part of the charm of Girtin's work. Like
Cozens he tended to draw in tone rather than local color,
using a prevailing key of warm gray (see Ill. 106).

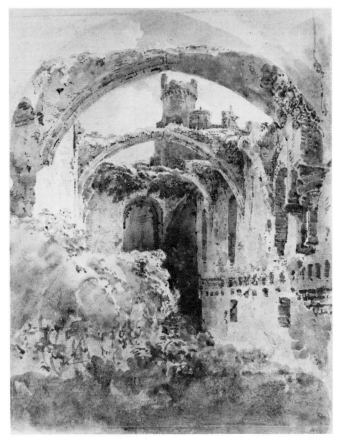

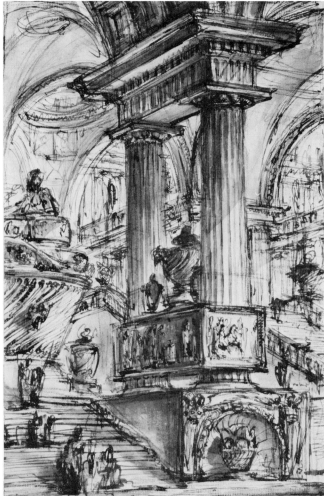

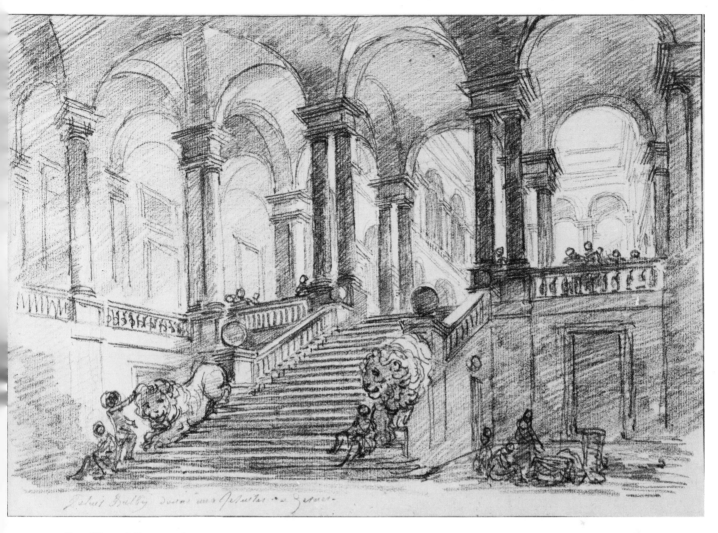

114. Jean Honoré Fragonard
Genoa, Staircase of the Palazzo Balbi

Fragonard, the supreme virtuoso of eighteenth-century French art, stayed in Italy from 1756 to 1761. He was very impressed by the work of Tiepolo. Fragonard's range was astonishing. Besides the frivolous *scènes galantes*, he could design equally well a composition in the Grand Manner. In this drawing (one of thousands by his hand) he reveals his complete mastery not only of the medium but also of perspective (aerial as well as linear). The coupled columns and arches gradually recede into the distance. The more distant are so delicately suggested as to be almost imperceptible. Throughout, the handling of the chalk has a freedom and spontaneity which gives a mood of light-hearted gaiety to the scene. Shadows are lightly scribbled in, and the whole atmosphere is theatrical but fun. This is so different from the oppressive, authoritative architecture of his contemporary, Piranesi.

OPPOSITE:
115. Giovanni Battista Piranesi
Monumental Staircase leading to a Vaulted Hall

Piranesi, architect, engraver, and etcher, went to Rome to study in 1740. This drawing, with its effect of massive grandeur and its sense of vaulted chambers and staircases extending even farther than the eye can see, is typical of his work. Although depending largely on line (a reflection of his etching technique), Piranesi also uses broad washes to create the breadth of shadow. His architectural inventions, especially his *Carceri d'Invenzione*, are labyrinthine interiors. Here staircases and archways endlessly interconnect with others, all suggesting a scale which dwarfs the human personality. Piranesi used perspective with skill and panache, apparently enjoying every opportunity of showing off his mastery of the subject. The repeating motif of massive urns creates an atmosphere of barbaric splendor.

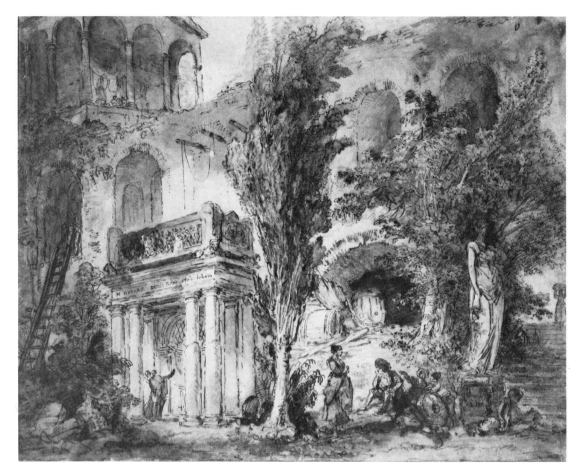

116. Hubert Robert
Rome, the Villa Ludovisi

Hubert Robert, a French painter also known as "Robert des ruines" was contemporary with Fragonard and Piranesi. From the age of 21 he also worked in Rome. Robert, influenced by Piranesi, produced many pictures of classical ruins. Some were real, some imaginary. While in Rome he became friendly with Fragonard and the two sometimes worked together. Each learned from and contributed to the style of the other. This drawing, with its abrupt changes of scale and viewpoint, produces by its inconsistencies a feeling of unreality. It suggests a collection of ideas rather than an actual location. It is a kind of *veduta ideata*: the scene is realistically conceived, but the elements appear to be imaginary. It would make a good setting for an eighteenth-century comedy in which the lovers exit or enter through such a variety of possibilities that endless confusion is caused. In short, it is a set – a romantic landscape garden with grottoes, ruins, and follies. It is not surprising that after Robert returned to Paris he was made Garden Designer to King Louis XVI.

117. Claude Lorrain
Landscape with Mercury and Argus

This pen and ink drawing is almost a prototype for the countless imitations made by artists from the seventeenth century to the present day. It is an example of the romantic approach in classical guise. It is classical in that the ostensible subject is drawn from Greek mythology and many aspects of the drawing may be said to be consistent with a classical approach. There is the pyramidal grouping of the figures, for example, and the reference to classical architecture. There is the emphasis on line and drawing, the underlying suggestion of a vertical/horizontal structure (the placing of figures and animals is on a horizontal line parallel to the picture plane), and the balanced composition (almost a trademark of Claude) with a vertical mass on each side joined by distant horizontals. But in spite of all these associations, the classical architecture is romantically ruined. The pastoral mood is much more important than Mercury and Argus. By his light touch and decorative treatment Claude suggests a kind of nostalgia for the past pleasures of the pagan world.

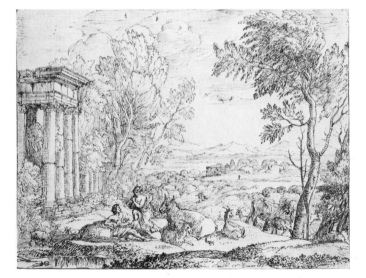

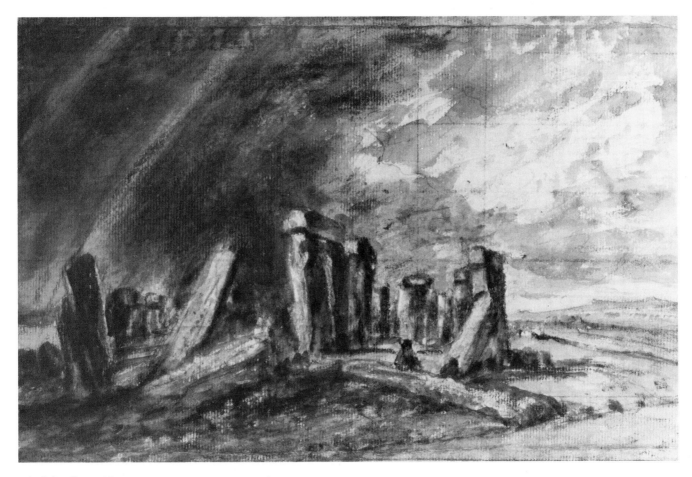

118. John Constable
Stonehenge

These two watercolors have much in common. The subject is ostensibly the building, redolent with history and ancient authority. Both drawings are, however, essentially romantic, and stress the mood rather than the subject matter. They recall Constable's words: "Painting is for me but another word for feeling." The drama of Stonehenge, an enigmatic tragedy, is played against a background of indigo sky. Where the sky is darkest, the hopeful light of the double rainbow appears all the more effective by contrast. After the death of his wife in 1828 Constable suffered long periods of depression: "I shall never feel again as I have felt," he said, "the face of the world is totally changed for me." His somberness was reflected in his work. The mood of his later landscapes is summed up in his own words: "Sudden and abrupt appearance of light, thunder clouds, wild autumnal evenings, solemn and shadowy twilight ... with variously tinted clouds, dark cold and grey, or ruddy and bright, with transitory gleams of light, even conflicts of the elements, to heighten if possible, the sentiment which belongs to a subject so awful and impressive." Constable made a special study of skies, which he described as "the chief organ of sentiment." In addition to setting down his own direct observations from Nature, he made copies of the schematic drawings which Alexander Cozens had made for his pupils.

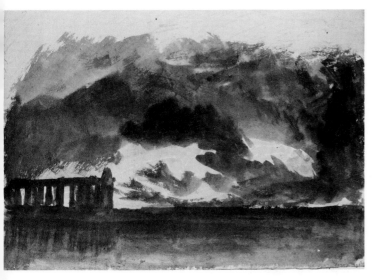

119. J. M. W. Turner
Paestum in a Storm

In this drawing of a skeletal building about to be devoured by the great sweep of anthropomorphic cloud, Turner, like Constable, makes use of the low eye-level to silhouette the temple against the skyline. This heightens the dramatic effect almost to the point of melodrama.

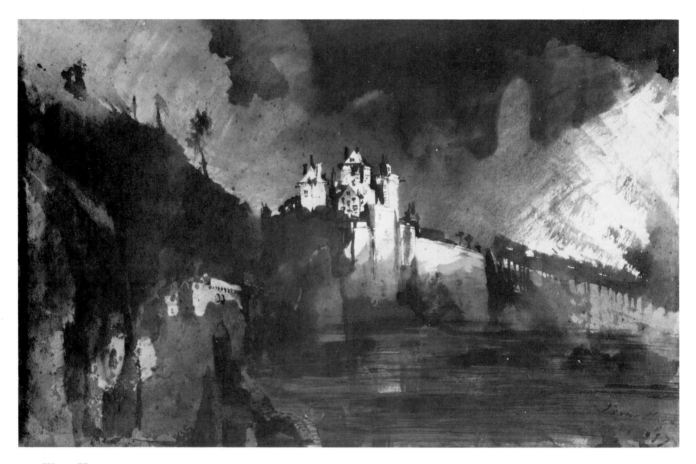

120. Victor Hugo
Castle above a Lake

This wash drawing is by Victor Hugo, the French writer, who is perhaps better known for his plays, novels, and poetry. As this drawing reveals, though, he was also an accomplished draftsman, and exemplifies the best of the Romantic tradition. The castle, its sheer walls towering above the dark water, is suddenly violently illuminated by the dazzling light source on the right. Thus, with all its drama and fairytale associations, the drawing is also an intriguing counterchange pattern. On the left we have the dark shape of the hill, creating a diagonal movement as it is silhouetted against the light sky. On the other side we have a blaze of light against a dark sky, throwing the central feature, the castle, into harsh relief. Everything seems to have been painted with a broad square brush and a great deal of confidence.

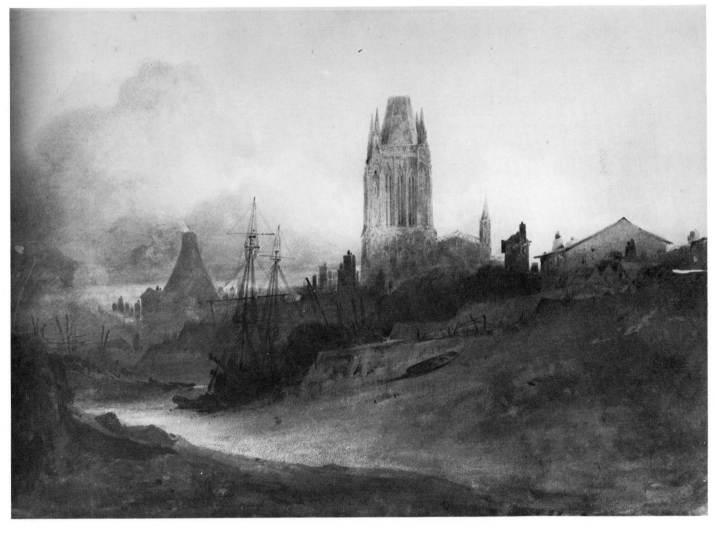

121. John Sell Cotman
Bristol, St Mary Redcliffe

Cotman, too, uses the device of silhouetting his shapes as a means of accentuating the dramatic mood so beloved by Romantics everywhere. The more we probe into the shadows the more we seem to be able to see. This is in spite of the mists which wreathe the scene in mystery. The broad simplicity of the design and the expressively silhouetted shapes are typical of this artist (see Ill. 105).

122. John Sell Cotman
A Sarcophagus in a Pleasure-ground

This watercolor illustrates Cotman's technique perfectly. His
use of the silhouetted, simplified shape can be seen in the
trees against the skyline. It is also seen in the changing tones
of the dead trunks as they are counterchanged against their
background – light against dark and vice versa. Cotman uses
very few colors. A cool blue-green contrasts with a warm
ochre. The two are mixed together to give an intermediate
warm olive-green. These, plus a unifying gray and a flat blue
wash for the sky, against which the clouds are silhouetted,
seem to be the only colors used. The result is a strong feeling
of pattern and unity of design, and a harmony of color
relationships.

OPPOSITE:
123. Richard Parkes Bonington
Paris, The Institut seen from the Quais

Bonington won a Gold Medal at the famous Salon of 1824
where his precocious talent (he was then 22) was admired by
Delacroix. Like Cotman, Bonington shows complete control
of his tonal and color schemes. His colors are based on muted
complementaries: a grayed-red and a gray leaning towards the
opposite of red – green. The tonal scheme is equally
controlled. Like Cotman, Bonington treats his shapes as
simple masses. The foreground uses a fairly wide range of
tone, from the light of the rock to the dark of the cast
shadows. In this foreground area we also find the most
positive color. In the middle distance, which consists of the
main building, we find the same colors repeated, but much
less assertive. As the colors become more subdued, the
tonal range is narrowed. In the distant scene the tonal
intervals are very close together (there is no contrast between
light and dark). The colors are also brought into close
relationship with each other, all tending towards a kind of
smoky blue. In this work all the elements – tone, color, and
placing – are beautifully and exactly controlled. The reds on
the rock and the position of the figure are examples of
Bonington's precision of placing. They evidence his
unsurpassed sense of composition. He died at 26 years of age.

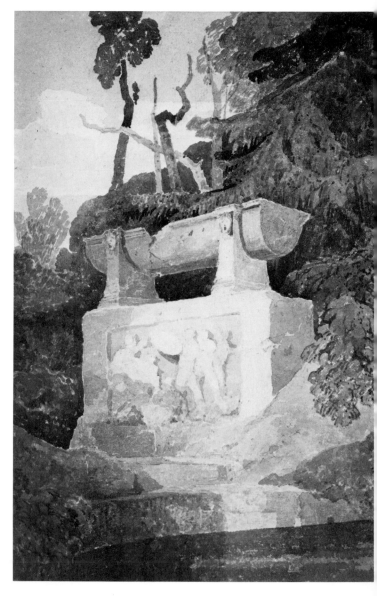

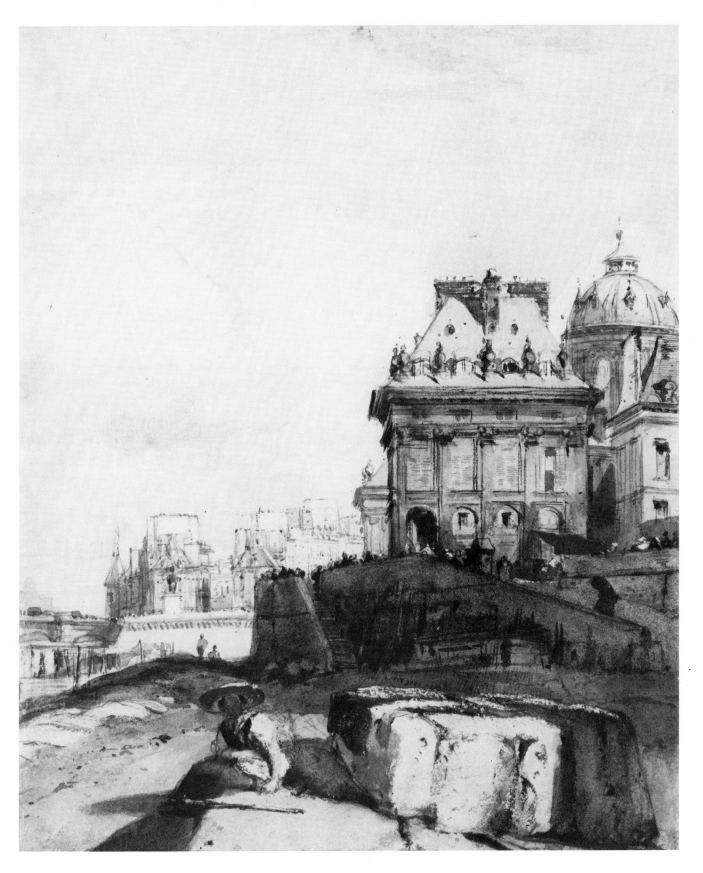

124. Vittore Carpaccio
Fortified Harbour with Shipping

Vittore Carpaccio painted a series of narrative pictures for the confraternities of his native city of Venice. The earliest and most influential was his *Legend of St Ursula* (1490-8), now in the Accademia, Venice. This drawing relates to the background of the scene entitled *St Ursula and the Prince taking leave of their Parents* (1495). If we study it closely we find that the subject has first been sketched lightly in red chalk and then revised and finalized in brown ink. Although light and shade are indicated on some of the buildings in a rather arbitrary way, there is no attempt to describe distance by using aerial perspective. Even the linear perspective is not at all consistent. In spite of this, Carpaccio has produced a drawing which has both a feeling of space, due to forms overlapping each other, and a sense of scale, due to detail being kept to the minimum. The combined effect of the restricted depth and the sense of structure (with the predominance of the horizontal and vertical) gives this work a very modern character.

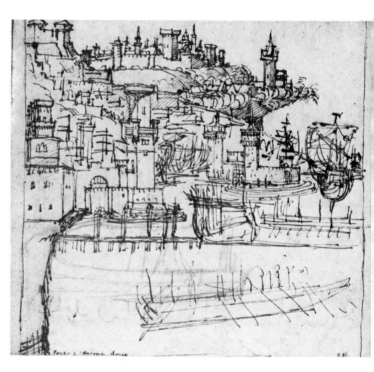

125. Jan van Scorel
Alpine Landscape with a Bridge

Contemporary with Vittore Carpaccio was the Dutch painter Jan van Scorel, known for his portraits and religious subjects. He traveled widely, visiting Germany, Italy, and perhaps the Holy Land. He would have had the opportunity to experience precipices and craggy cliffs first hand. In this pen-and-ink drawing linear perspective is as inconsistent as in Carpaccio's (note, for example, the house on the bridge). But van Scorel does use a light tone of ink for the view through the arch of the bridge. The distant scene, by coincidence, fits into the archway exactly! The rocky promontories and the buildings perched upon them are also treated with a degree of aerial perspective. Lines become progressively fainter as one form consistently, almost inevitably, overlaps the next. The spiky character of this drawing with its turrets and towers belongs more to the medieval world than to the Renaissance (compare Ill. 59).

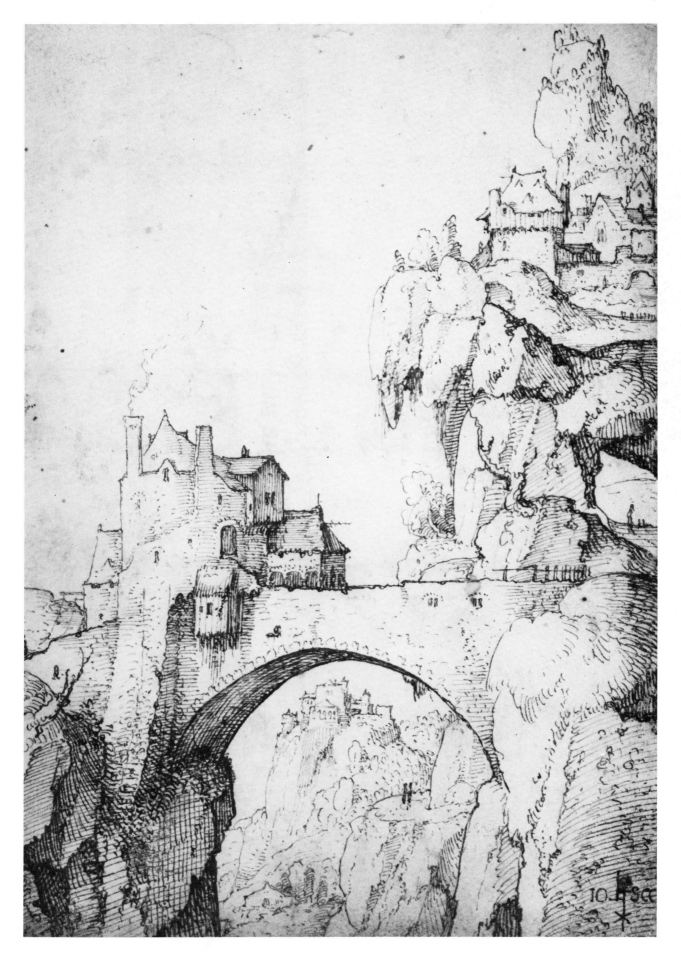

It was said in the Introduction to this section that perspective, being more evident in buildings than in other subjects, might pose some problems, though not for the competent artist. But in this drawing by Cézanne – a more than competent artist – we will find it very difficult to discover the eye-level, or indeed a vanishing point for any of the lines of these buildings. Even where we have a three-quarter view of a building the receding wall is rotated toward us so that its lines lie parallel with the picture plane rather than disappearing towards the eye-level. Cézanne makes use of all the lines he can find which are parallel to the picture plane. Those are lines which are horizontal or vertical or which can be made to fit into such a format. The resulting drawing tells us nothing about light and shade, the time of day or direction of light, the tonal value of colors, or the species of trees. It is a drawing solely about structure. Space is not expressed by traditional linear perspective but is *represented* by a series of steps. Each step is parallel to the picture plane. It is a new pictorial concept, dealing in finding visual equivalents for space rather than creating illusions of space by using perspective and aerial perspective. Cézanne's revolutionary ideas were to have widespread repercussions.

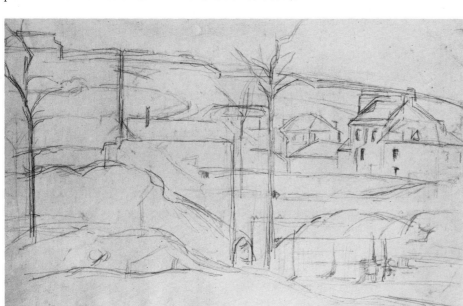

126. Paul Cézanne
Provençal Landscape with Trees and Houses

127. Piet Mondrian
Church at Domburg, 1914

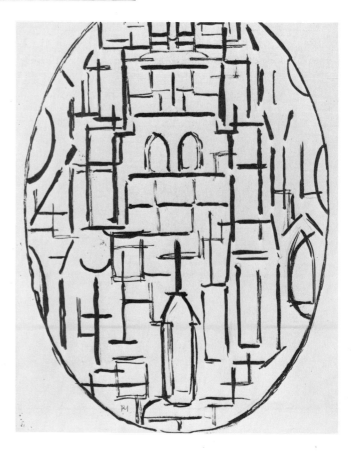

Mondrian's early works (*c.* 1890-1900) show the influence of Dutch naturalism and of Corot. In the early years of this century he became more interested in light and the Impressionists, and a little later experimented with Pointillism, Fauvism, and Expressionism. But by 1908 he was beginning to find his own way. In that year Mondrian first went to Domburg, a village to which he returned many times. Here he began work on his Tree series: an apple tree gradually reduced to a set of vertical and horizontal lines (see Ill. 95). He evolved a method of systematically eliminating all detail from a subject, reducing color to a minimum, while concentrating on expressing the basic linear structure. In this drawing of the parish church Mondrian has applied the same technique. It is easy to recognize the various parts – the porch, the windows, and the cruciform sign. The sketch is, above all, essentially architectural in its basic rhythms. Mondrian's drawings of this period, with their emphasis on vertical/horizontal relationships, anticipate one of the fundamental elements of Neoplasticism – the ultimate reduction to the vertical and horizontal, to the total exclusion of all other lines.

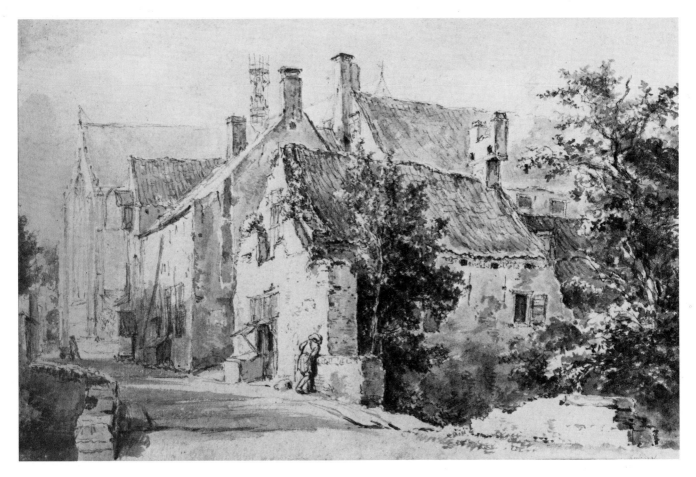

128. Jacob van Ruysdael
View in Alkmaar with the Groote Kerk

The two Dutch artists whose work is illustrated here were roughly contemporaries. Ruysdael specialized in landscapes while Saenredam specialized in church interiors. Ruysdael was the more influential (Hobbema was his pupil), and Gainsborough, Constable, and the Barbizon school owed much to his example. In fact Ruysdael's drawing reminds us of drawings by Constable. The same loving attention is paid to the individual character of crumbling stone and old brickwork. There is the same mood of quiet acceptance and understanding. It is a drawing by a native who loves what he sees. The composition Ruysdael has chosen is unusual in that it moves from right to left. Tone is used both to express color (the dark colored trees and the roofs of the houses are clearly a darker color than the walls) and to express shadow, the effect of light and shade. In addition, tone is used with great skill to express aerial perspective.

129. Pieter Jansz Saenredam
Interior of the So-called Chapel Church at Alkmaar

The cold austerity of this drawing by Saenredam reminds us of the preliminary sketches from an architect's office. The washes are very skillfully handled, the perspective is immaculate, and everything is very neat, clean, and precise.

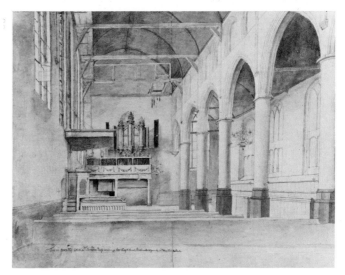

Animals

"Animals are good to know for having no education they are free of prejudice." DEGAS

Animals have been a popular subject for artists from prehistoric times. This is hardly surprising as they have played a vital role in Man's development, feeding and clothing him, befriending him, working at his side, and threatening his life. For the artist they represent a special challenge. To capture their swift movement he must choose a medium which enables him to respond quickly with hand and eye – pen and ink, chalk, or charcoal. Doing justice to their immensely varied characteristics demands close observation and attention to detail. In one case it may be essential to express the coiled muscles, or, in another, the direction of hair growth, speed of reaction, grace of movement or sense of brute force.

Animals have represented something different to each society. The Ancient Egyptians went so far as to represent their gods in animal form. If we take just one case, that of the horse (perhaps the most rewarding subject for the artist) we can see that changing attitudes to animals are clearly reflected in the way they have been represented in art. The Greeks treated the horse with almost the same reverence as the human figure. To the Romans, the horse was a kind of throne to set off an emperor or general – the equestrian monument captured the proud, powerful nature of both horse and rider. During the ensuing Dark Ages all kinds of curious and unlikely little beasts (some crawling out from the subconscious) entwined themselves around initial letters and decorated the borders of manuscripts. Combinations of different animals' parts appear as dragons and gargoyles, assembled as if by alchemy. The armored war horse, which first appeared in the Middle Ages, represented a new development. It was trained to use its hooves in a kind of equine karate. This animal features in the works of the early Renaissance artist, Paolo Uccello (for example *The Rout of San Romano*).

The re-awakening interest in nature during the Renaissance resulted in a realistic study of animals and their anatomy. Leonardo da Vinci, the endless experimenter, made numerous drawings of the horse: as a monument, as a study of comparative anatomy and facial expression, and as part of his exploration of movement. It was during the Baroque period, however, that artists used the sweeping curve of horses' necks, manes, and rounded rumps to convey the robust, powerful mood of the age. In the nineteenth century the horse became a whole series of subjects in itself. Géricault and Delacroix both saw the horse as a powerful symbol of Romanticism. To Toulouse-Lautrec and Degas the horse was part of everyday life. Horse and rider were drawn as part of the social scene, but we were also taken behind the scenes, literally, to the sweat and sawdust of the circus. Degas was one of the first to make use of the research into animal movement by the pioneer photographer Eadweard Muybridge. His photography of motion (almost cine-photography) showed artists, for the first time, the position of the horse's legs when in motion.

Given the immense scope of the subject it is perhaps not so surprising that many of the world's great draftsmen have found the animal a source of inspiration, and that their interpretations have been so diverse. Rembrandt's lions are leonine, where Rubens' are Rubenesque. Watteau's greyhounds and Fragonard's bull all share the elegance of the eighteenth-century Rococo. The animals of Stubbs are anatomically correct. As for today, Picasso has given us a whole repertoire of interchangeable roles played by the bull, horse, and man, conveying all the inevitability of classical tragedy.

OPPOSITE ABOVE:

Prehistoric Man depended on large herds of animals for food and clothing, and for tools and weapons, which he made from bones. Hoping to ensure a successful hunt, he drew his prey on the limestone walls of caves, incorporating cracks and using the naturally rounded surfaces where they could be helpful in expressing the form. The technique often consists (as here) of a strong outline in black drawn by brush (a chewed-out stick or stiff bristle brush), filled in with areas of color, possibly using a pad of fur.

Paleolithic artists were familiar with the animals depicted. They expressed their characteristics of grace, strength or swiftness with a skill and conviction which, strangely enough, was not seen again until thousands of years later. This example shows an appreciation of the bull bisons' strength and agility as they stand poised ready for instant action. The massive forequarters and formidable bulk stress the latent power and dangerous potentiality of the beasts. The drawing was made by an artist who had felt the earth shake under the pounding hooves of creatures like these. It reveals such an intimate knowledge. It also reveals an attention to perspective in the use of the three-quarter view. The way in which the rumps overlap conveys convincingly a sense of space.

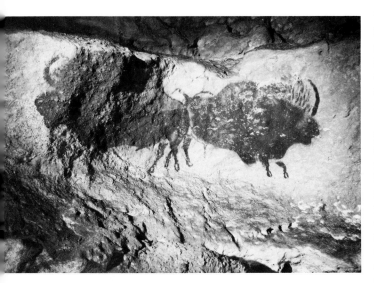

130. Two Bison, back to back
(early Magdalenian period)

131. Pablo Picasso
Minotaur Attacking an Amazon

The minotaur, the archetypal union of man and beast, is seen in Picasso's personal mythology in a whole repertoire of changing roles. It ranges from the seducer to the reveler, from the sacrificial beast in the microcosm of the bullring, facing the moment of truth, to the bull/man, blinded and deprived of brute strength, led by an innocent little girl along the sea-shore.

In this work the bull/man (man's animal nature) is seen as a powerful representation of animal lust. It is the ancient Beauty and Beast theme. The drawing is carried out in a combined medium, etching and aquatint. The etched lines are paralleled by the sugar lift aquatint line, a technique which reiterates and reinforces the linear image. All the lines are very closely confined within the available space, a device which emphasizes the power of the animal in contrast to the smallness of the cage. The lines are all drawn with an undulating movement which is again emphasized by the contrast with the minor movement of the lines representing the curly body hairs. The whole lunging rush starts from the position of the foot, pushing against the corner of the frame. Essentially this is a design involving a major diagonal thrust from left to right, opposed by a minor movement represented by the restraining hand of the victim. All the lines in this drawing are interconnected, resulting in a set of complex interweaving lines rather than a depiction of separate protagonists. The bull's head and the female hand are one line. The horn fits the fingers, the fingertips are on the shoulder line, and the plunging hooves (echoes of the bullring) exactly fit into the line of the minotaur's leg.

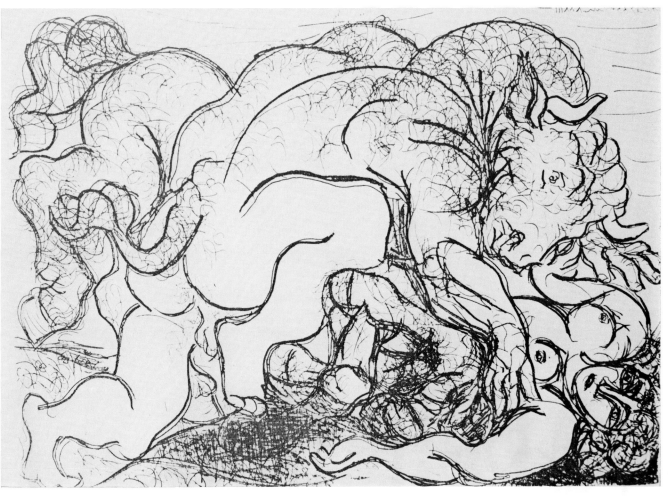

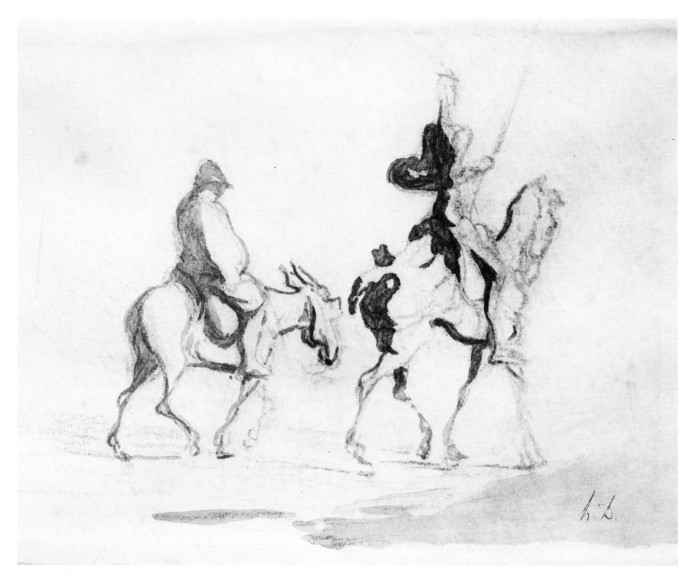

132. Honoré Daumier
Don Quixote and Sancho Panza

Daumier was a caricaturist as well as a gifted draftsman, who specialized in a few subjects. In a great many of his works, however, the real subject is *tone*. In fact he often reduces the image to very simple tones indeed. In this case he has used charcoal and black ink to produce a drawing in virtually two tones. The charcoal supplies only a slight suggestion of halftone between the extremes of white and black.

There is an amusing relationship between the portly, bowed figures of Sancho Panza and his donkey, and the aristocratic, upright Don Quixote and his bony nag: a gentle gibe by Daumier at the heroic pair.

133. Pablo Picasso
The Picador

Picasso, using the similar medium of brush and wash, expresses no mockery, only harsh reality. Using short bursts of line at opposing angles and with tremendous vigor, he produces an example of calligraphic shorthand. The brush, sometimes fully loaded and sometimes starved before the stroke is complete, produces a broken effect (see Rembrandt's

A Girl Sleeping, Ill. 40). We can feel the way the brush bucked and twisted in Picasso's hand as it was called upon to execute the abrupt twists reminiscent of the violent subject. The resulting harsh contrast of black and white suggests the sun and the drama.

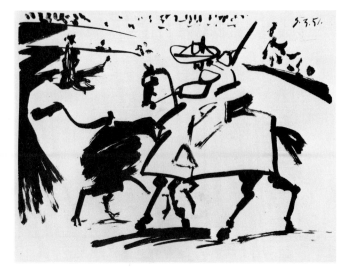

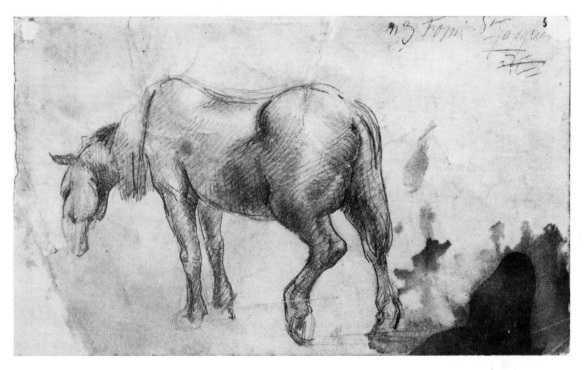

134. Paul Cézanne
The Tired Horse

Cézanne treats this animal in much the same way as a still-life of apples. He was not concerned to draw the horse as a symbol of freedom (like Géricault), or as a throne for a general, or as a seat for a jockey. Cézanne wanted to find, as in all his work, a means of conveying his idea of *form*. The drawing is carried out in pencil using directional hatching to indicate tone, the chief means Cézanne uses to convey the feeling of form. This hatching is always across the forms, curved lines being used over rounder forms, straight lines on flattened forms. By using a heavier and richer hatching technique on the rump, Cézanne brings the hindquarters nearer. The contour lines are broken and subtly varied – sometimes overlapping, sometimes revised – but never defining or confirming the forms by their edges. The belly, basically cylindrical, is treated as a series of planes. By changing the direction of strokes and merging the tones with his fingers, Cézanne alters the angles of the planes. Of particular importance in helping to establish the form of the belly is the emphasis placed on those lines which separate belly and legs. The downward line over the head is similarly emphasized by the drooping lines of the mane.

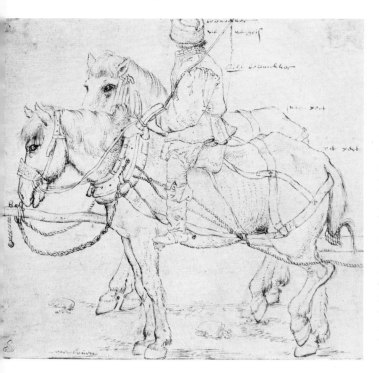

135. Pieter Bruegel the Elder
The Team of Horses

In this carefully observed study of horses in their harness, Bruegel conveys by the stance and carriage of the head the enforced patience of the animal. Using the medium of pen and ink over a preliminary chalk drawing, Bruegel uses a wide variety of lines to express the different textures. The hair falling over the eyes is shown as a series of flowing parallels. The curling mane pushed forward by the halter becomes springing curves. The longer hairs on the back of the legs and the shorter hairs on the front are differentiated by linear interpretations. Short broken lines, and lines of dots, are used not only to suggest the all-over body hair, but to express the underlying anatomical structure of bone and muscle. We see the rib cage, the bony structure of the pelvis, and the main muscle masses clearly modeled by this linear means. Furthermore, by using the carefully observed lines of the harness as it fits around and over the body, Bruegel conveys a strong sense of form as well as texture.

136. Leonardo da Vinci
Studies of Horsemen

Both Leonardo and Klee were particularly interested in the study of movement. Leonardo made drawings of currents of water, studying flow patterns under different conditions and comparing their fluid rhythms with those he found in his studies of the directional growth of hair, roots, and foliage. These little sketches of galloping horses, carried out in a kind of shorthand, allow us to look over Leonardo's shoulder as he visually *thinks aloud* about the possibilities of expressing violent action through the horse-and-rider theme. All these small-scale dramatic events are depicted in the minimum number of lines. Leonardo made many detailed studies of human and animal anatomy, enabling him to summarize their appearance concisely from any viewpoint.

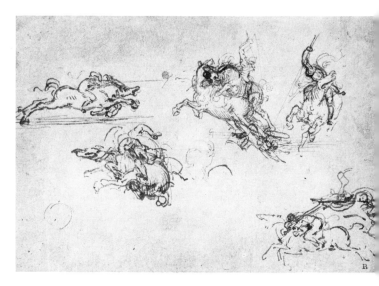

137. Paul Klee
Galloping Horses

Klee, too, was interested in all forms of movement, finding linear equivalents (rather than visual descriptions) for all kinds of motion. This included the movements of the conductor's baton at concerts – he was passionately interested in music. His approach to galloping horses is somewhat different from that of Leonardo. It is the moving line itself which is really the subject of Klee's drawing. This is not really a drawing of a galloping horse seen in three positions (Klee's titles are often misleading!), but of galloping *lines*. In his teaching and in his own work Klee examined the nature of line, discovering which lines were swift or slow, and which other qualities they could express. In this drawing continuous lines create an enclosed space within which smaller continuous movements revolve. The combined head/neck feature, with its phallic overtones, breaks out from this continuity, thereby emphasizing it.

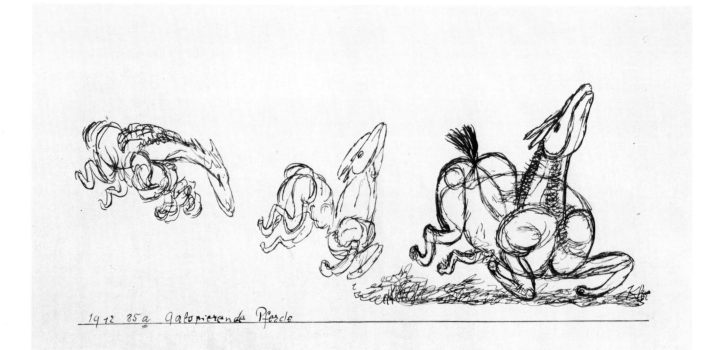

138. Albrecht Dürer
Death on Horseback

Dürer, like Leonardo da Vinci, made many detailed studies of horses and mounted knights. He was very familiar with equine anatomy. But here he freely invents and exaggerates in order to produce this disturbingly convincing image of Death on horseback (which was possibly inspired by an outbreak of plague in Dürer's home town in the same year, 1505). These creatures of skin and bone, joints swollen and distorted, advance with a kind of sinister inevitability – a curiously plodding, staggering gait suggested by the distance between the animal's splayed back legs.

Dürer was a very skillful engraver and in fact used all media with equal facility. Here he shows complete control over the charcoal, varying the strength of the line from faint to dark in order to suggest modeling. The animal's ribs are gradually strengthened in tone as they pass into shadow under the belly. Similarly, the line used to describe the protruding bones of the animal's pelvis begins very faintly and then swoops into a dark, wide line, creating the bony hollow, as Dürer increases the pressure.

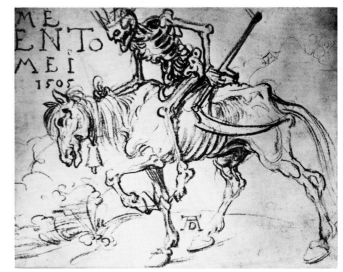

139. Eugène Delacroix
Tiger Attacking a Wild Horse

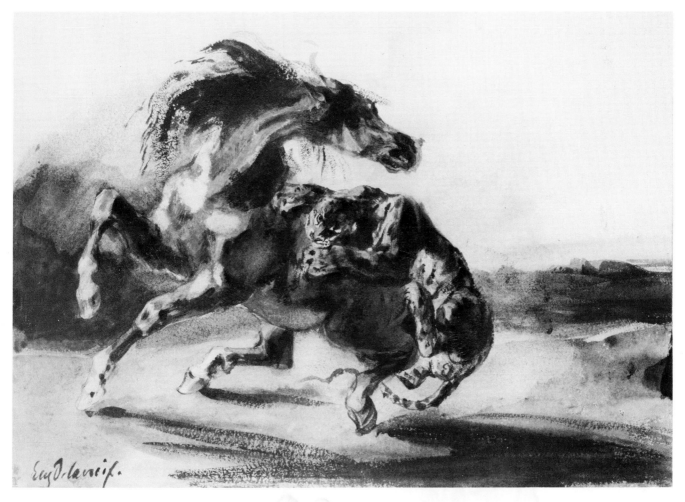

Of the various conflicting art movements which arose during the nineteenth century, Romanticism was the most dramatic. In the forefront of this movement was Delacroix, who, like all Romantic artists, saw the horse as the spirit of untamed freedom. The horse represents a wild creature roaming where it chooses, free as the wind. In the Romantic drama depicted here, a wild, desolate landscape is indicated by a few strokes of color dragged over an initial wash. The flying mane of the horse is similarly expressed. It emphasizes the tremendously vigorous turn of the horse's head and muscular neck. Delacroix creates the sheen on the coat and rippling muscles of this elegant animal by making the most of reflected lights. Notice, for example, the wetting and wiping out of the wash under the belly and on the forequarters.

140. Theodore Géricault
Charging Officer of the Carabineers

Here we have two drawings stressing the idea of movement. One is a three-quarter back view, the other a three-quarter front view. Both rely on perspective as a means of creating space within which the form can move. Géricault uses black chalk to draw the shape, bringing the hindquarters nearer by strengthening these lines. The drawing is then tinted with watercolor, silhouetting the rider against the sky. The low horizon line and the accent on sweeping curves create a sense of the heroic. The movement is swashbuckling and slightly larger than life. The officer becomes his own equestrian monument, caught in a momentary pause before the charge.

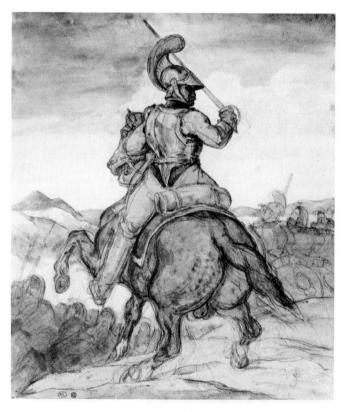

141. Henri de Toulouse-Lautrec
Equestrienne

Toulouse-Lautrec presents us with a ringside view of his equestrienne. Again perspective is emphasized, throwing the animal's massive head and the exaggerated curve of its powerful neck into close-up. This creates a strong contrast with the petite figure of the equestrienne, who effortlessly controls her mount while gently restraining the rise and fall of her transparent gauze skirts. Toulouse-Lautrec uses the outline of the trappings (in a similar way to Bruegel) to define the forms by cross-section.

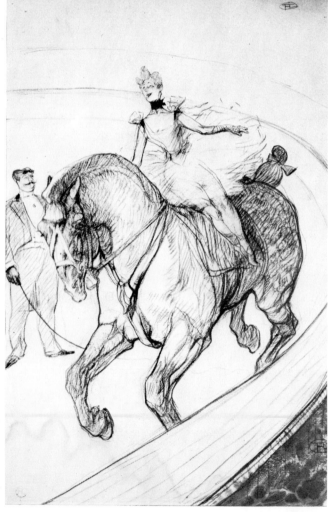

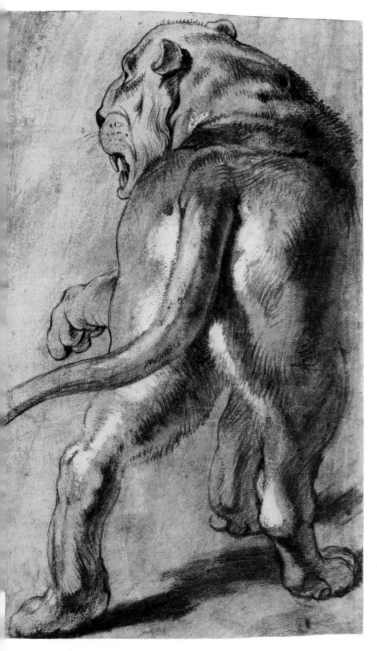

142. Peter Paul Rubens
Lioness

Rubens' lioness, a study for a painting of Daniel in the Lions' Den, is typical of Rubens and of the Baroque period. Using the paper as a mid-tone, Rubens skillfully describes the form and direction of hair growth by means of closely hatched lines. The back view – the curves of the bottom accentuated by the white highlights, and the serpentine curves of the swinging tail emphasizing the feeling of movement – is typical of the Baroque. In this drawing the foreshortening is not very convincing. The animal's head is too large for the position in which it is described. One feels that this is a skillful piece of drawing from memory.

143. Rembrandt
Four Studies of Lions

Like his drawings of elephants, Rembrandt's studies of lions (perhaps done in preparation for his etching of St Jerome) are clearly drawn from life. They walk, recline or doze with heavy head resting on paws, in that deceptively lazy *pussy-cat* way so typical of the animal. They are all expressed with Rembrandt's characteristic economy. Minimum means are used to convey maximum expressiveness. There is little or no need to say anything more about this work – the drawing says it all.

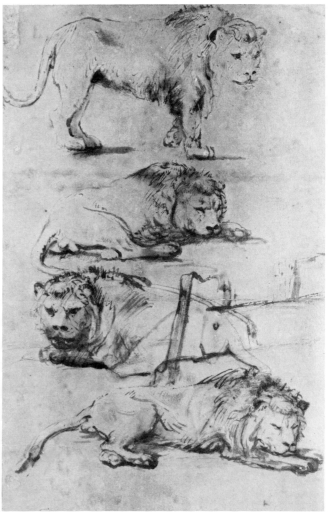

144. Theodore Géricault
Studies of a Wild Striped Cat

Since the worship of the cat as a deity in Ancient Egypt, many artists have been fascinated by the creature's lithe grace. These studies of a cat by Géricault, in sharp but soft pencil, are crisp, sure, and full of observed detail. However, the detail is kept subordinate to the more general idea of the feline form and character of the animal. Géricault varies the strength of the pencil-work considerably in different parts of these studies, making his line as expressive as possible. Generally, the nearer parts are made darker in order to bring them closer. He also uses the pencil to suggest the color and pattern of the coat. The dark patches are used very much to draw the form as well as to express the marking. Notice the detailed attention paid to eye-sockets and the way the pencil suggests the color of drawn-back lips.

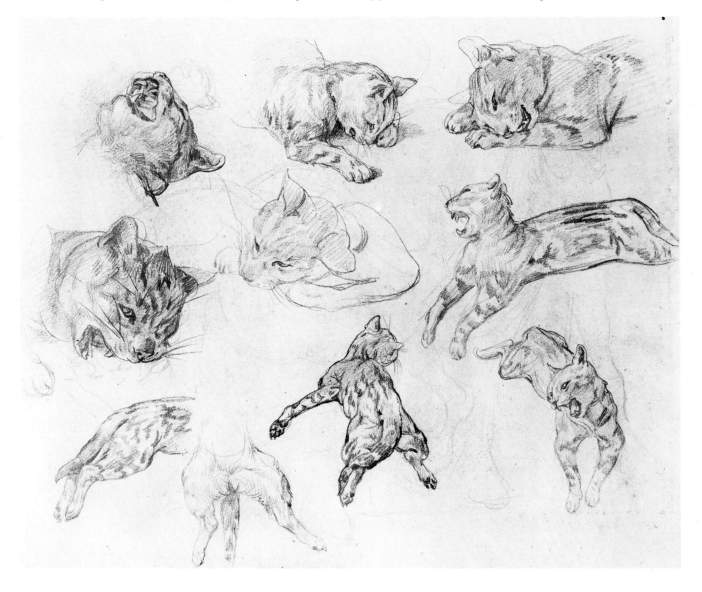

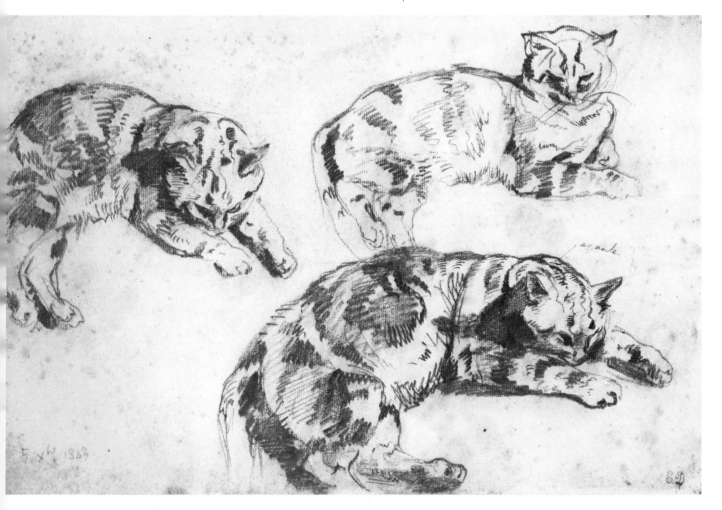

145. Eugène Delacroix
Three Studies of Cats

Delacroix's three studies are quite different in emphasis and intention. There is very little detail. Delacroix places much more emphasis on tone than Géricault, who favors a comparatively linear approach. The patches of loosely scribbled crayon create a pattern of light and dark areas which effectively communicate a vision of the lazy domesticated animal with its underlying independence of character.

Here are two very different approaches to a similar subject. Francis Barlow's approach is that of the engraver, using a clear, precise line (although the artist is not quite so clear about what to do with the rhino's front legs!). For all its clarity, though, it is obvious that Barlow did not make this study of a so-called battle from life. Rembrandt, with all the imprecision of his outlines, clearly drew his elephant from direct observation, the little group of onlookers in the background supplying a sense of scale. Francis Barlow may have seen the stuffed head of an elephant, since it appears more elephantine than the body. But the rest is based on verbal description. The rhinoceros was presumably described as *armored*. So the artist has dressed it in suitably adapted fashionable armor of his own time. The tailpiece is particularly inventive, as are the *Bermuda shorts* for the back legs. Similarly, we are to understand that an elephant is a wrinkled beast with flat feet and five toes. The wrinkles depicted by Barlow do little to describe the form but ripple all over the surface, suggesting a mass of quivering jelly. Rembrandt, on the other hand, uses the chalk to produce a coarse-grained effect which expresses the leathery texture of the animal's skin. By creating an involved network of directional hatching, Rembrandt gives not only a feeling of texture but also a feeling of form. The lines used to indicate the wrinkles of skin are at the same time suggestive both of the sections of form and of the folds of flesh. (The study was possibly a preparation for the elephant in the background of the Adam and Eve etching of 1638.)

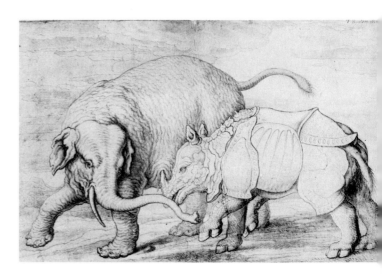

146. Francis Barlow
Fight between an Elephant and Rhinoceros

147. Rembrandt
Elephant

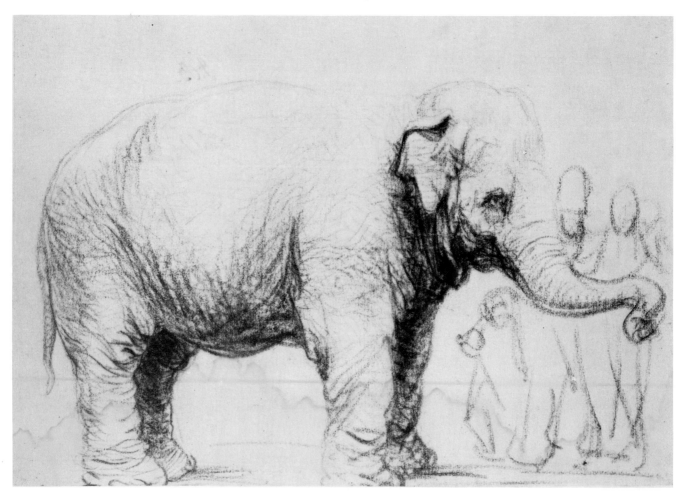

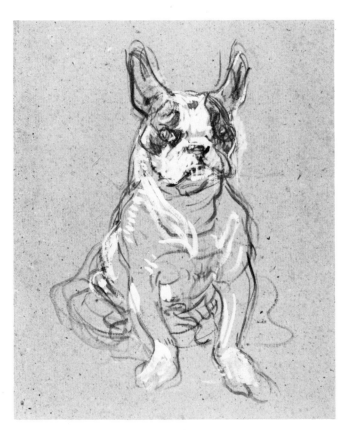

148. Henri de Toulouse-Lautrec
Bouboule, Madame Palmyre's Bulldog

Sometimes Toulouse-Lautrec's drawings remind us of those of Daumier (see Ill. 132). Both artists were essentially draftsmen, both lithographers, and both had a feeling for caricature. The pugnacious pose of the bulldog, with curved ears echoing the curves of its bandy legs, displays very skillful handling of the brush. Toulouse-Lautrec often worked on a toned ground (straw board or brown paper), using light and dark strokes and leaving the ground as the middle tone. As we study the drawing we begin to notice how much of it consists of the untouched paper! The drawing is made up of a number of swift assessments of the relative positions of selected lines of the pose. These lines are then revised and finalized by drawing other, stronger versions on top.

149. Albrecht Dürer
Greyhound

Dürer uses the brush just as skillfully in his drawing of a greyhound. But Dürer's method is different from Toulouse-Lautrec's. We see here the linear approach of the engraver. We feel his complete control of the brush as he creates lines which start almost imperceptibly, gradually swell and strengthen, thicken to express shadows, and fade away again. These curving parallel lines express the modeling of the surface, the direction of hair growth, and the textures of different areas.

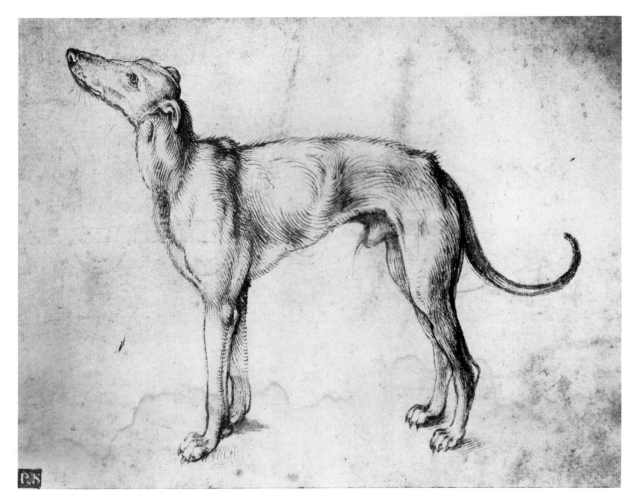

150. François Boucher
Study of a Rooster

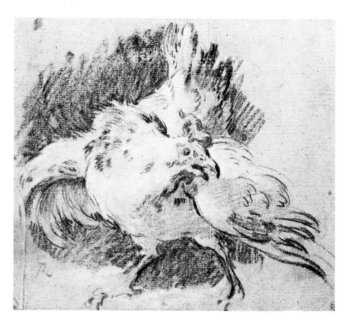

Boucher's *Study of a Rooster* and Fragonard's *Bull in a Stable* may seem at first sight a rather unlikely pair with very little in common. But both drawings share characteristics of the fashionable Rococo style favored by the decorative artists of eighteenth-century France. The waving comb of the rooster, the emphatic curves of the bull's horns, and the double curve of its tail — all contribute to the overall decorative quality of these drawings.

The rooster, its comb and face colored red, is effectively made up of decoratively sweeping curves. The outstretched wings and ruffled feathers are treated (appropriately enough) with feathery strokes of the chalk. This technique can also be seen in Watteau's dromedary (see Ill. 153) and in the depiction of trees during this period (see Ill. 90). The bull, although carried out in a different medium, bistre wash, shows much the same kind of feathery handling as the bird. The silhouetted edges of the animal's ears are quite feathered. Indeed the whole drawing, like that of the rooster, is carried out in a series of rippling curves which convey a curious sense of prettiness, somewhat at variance with the animal's massive form.

151. Jean Honoré Fragonard
Bull in a Stable

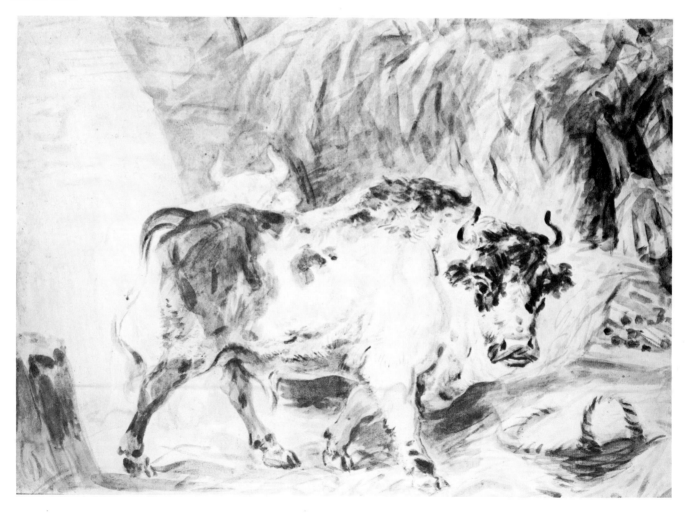

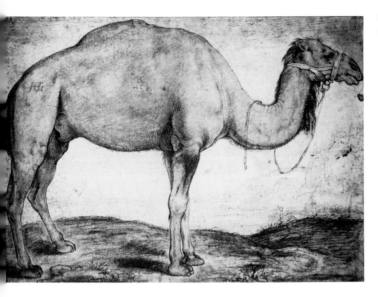

152. Hendrick Goltzius
Camel

Goltzius was a Dutch engraver and painter. From about 1600 his paintings were much influenced by Italian mannerism. As an engraver he is noted for the way in which he exploited all the tonal possibilities of line. Surface qualities were emphasized by thickening or swelling the engraved lines. This camel is essentially linear in treatment. From the looped rein over the beast's neck, the whole form is bounded by a precise and clearly observed outline. Within this outline the surface is subtly modeled by gradations of the red and black chalk.

153. Jean Antoine Watteau
Five Studies of a Dromedary

Watteau's chalk studies of a dromedary look almost feathery by comparison. The tufts of hair on the shoulders and elegantly curling beard are typical of the Rococo artist's interest in the decorative (see Ills. 56 and 90). The feeling of form is created by the close directional hatching generally traveling across the shorter direction of the form.

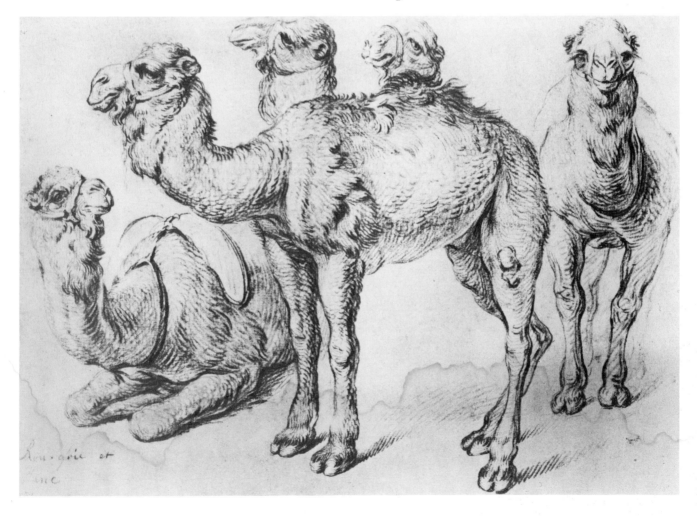

Further Reading

Anthony Bertram, *One Thousand Years of Drawing* (Studio Vista, 1966)

Jean Cassou and P. H. Jaccottet, *French Drawing of the 20th Century* (Thames and Hudson, 1955)

Fred Dubery and John Willats, *Drawing Systems* (Studio Vista, 1972)

Colin T. Eisler, *German Drawings: From the 15th Century to the Expressionists,* "Great Drawings of the World" series (Studio Vista, 1965)

E. H. Gombrich, *Art and Illusion* (Phaidon Press, 2nd edition 1977)

Una E. Johnson, *20th Century Drawings: Part 1 1900–1940,* "Great Drawings of the World" series (Weidenfeld and Nicholson, 1964)

Una E. Johnson, *20th Century Drawings: From 1940 to the Present Day,* "Great Drawings of the World" series (Studio Vista, 1965)

Frederick Malins, *Understanding Pictures: Elements of Composition* (Phaidon Press, 1979)

Master Draftsman Series (over thirty titles): the drawings of the great artists (Borden Publishing Company, Alhambra, California, 1966)

Philip Rawson, *Drawing,* "The Appreciation of the Arts" No. 3 (Oxford University Press, 1969)

A. G. Reynolds, *Nineteenth Century Drawings* (Pleiades Art Books, 1949)

Jakob Rosenberg, *Great Draughtsmen from Pisanello to Picasso* (Oxford University Press, 1959)

Benjamin Rowland, Jr., *Cave to Renaissance,* "Great Drawings of the World" series (Studio Vista, 1965)

Regina Schoolman and Charles E. Slatkin, *Six Centuries of French Master Drawings in America* (Oxford University Press, 1950)

Jean Vallery-Radot, *French Drawings: From the 15th to the Early 19th Century.* "Great Drawings of the World" series (Studio Vista, 1965)

PICTURE ACKNOWLEDGEMENTS

The author and publishers would like to thank the following individuals and institutions for supplying photographs: Bildarchiv Preussischer Kulturbesitz (Ills. 13, 109), Courtauld Institute of Art (37), Giraudon (79), Robert E. Mates (82), The Museum of Modern Art, New York (18), and The Art Museum, Princeton University (3); illustrations 2, 11a, b, 14, 15, 20, 25, 31, 33, 35, 36, 39, 40, 43, 44, 48, 50, 58, 59, 62–5, 70, 71, 76, 80, 84–90, 92, 93, 98–100, 102–7, 110–25, 128, 129, 136, 138, 142, 143, 147, 152 are reproduced by Courtesy of the Trustees of the British Museum.
Illustrations 24, 51, 140 are Clichés des Musées Nationaux, Paris; 130 is © Arch. Phot. Paris/S.P.A.D.E.M.. Fig. 1 first appeared in *Remembering: A Study in Experimental and Social Psychology* by F. C. Bartlett (Cambridge University Press, 1932), and is reproduced by permission of the publishers.